U.S. COINS BY DESIGN TYPES

Q. David Bowers

U.S. Coins by Design Types

An Action Guide for the Collector and Investor

by
Q. David Bowers

Bowers and Merena Galleries, Inc.

Other reference books by Q. David Bowers:

Coins and Collectors, United States Half Cents 1793-1857, Early American Car Advertisements, Put Another Nickel In, Guidebook of Automatic Musical Instruments—Vol. I, Guidebook of Automatic Musical Instruments—Vol. II, How to be a Successful Coin Dealer, Encyclopedia of Automatic Musical Instruments, How to Start a Coin Collection, Collecting Rare Coins for Profit, A Tune for a Token, Adventures With Rare Coins, The History of United States Coinage (for The Johns Hopkins University), *Treasures of Mechanical Music* (with Art Reblitz), *The Postcards of Alphonse Mucha* (with Mary Martin), *Robert Robinson: American Illustrator, Common Sense Coin Investment, Official ANA Grading Standards for U.S. Coins* (Introduction), *United States Gold Coins: An Illustrated History, Virgil Brand: The Man and His Era, Abe Kosoff: Dean of Numismatics, The Moxie Encyclopedia, United States Copper Coins: An Action Guide for the Collector and Investor, U.S. Three-Cent and Five-Cent Coins: An Action Guide for the Collector and Investor, Nickelodeon Theatres and Their Music, The Strange Career of Dr. Wilkins, Muriel Ostriche: Princess of Silent Films, The Norweb Collection: An American Legacy* (with Michael Hodder), *The Numismatist's Bedside Companion, High Profits From Rare Coin Investment, The Numismatist's Fireside Companion,* and *How to be a Successful Coin Dealer* (revised edition).

BOWERS AND MERENA GALLERIES, INC.
Box 1224
Wolfeboro, NH 03894
(603) 569-5095

Catalogues Issued
Sales by Mail Only
(All coins are kept in bank vaults)

Second Edition, 1989
ISBN: 0-943161-13-4

Contents

CREDITS

Typesetting and much of the production work for the book was done by Margaret Graf. Proofreading, layout, and graphics work were by the Graphics Arts Department of Bowers & Merena Galleries, Inc., including Jane McCabe, Linda Heilig, Sarah Whitten-French, and Jane Fernald. Photography was by Anne Hassin and Cathy Dumont.

Thomas J. Becker, Dr. Richard A. Bagg, Ray Merena and Doreen Richards helped with data and research information. Thanks also to the United States Mint and the American Numismatic Society.

Additional credits for the second edition, 1989.

For the second edition, the present work has been slightly revised to incorporate suggestions of readers, including some valuable comments submitted by Ruben Flores. The second edition features a chapter not in the earlier edition, chapter 12, "Some Interesting Options."

Appreciation is expressed to the following Bowers and Merena staff members who have helped with corrections and typography for the revised edition: Richard A. Bagg, Ph.D., Lee Blythe Lilljedahl, William Winter, Linda Heilig, Judy Bouchard, and Roberta French.

About the Author

Q. David Bowers, an owner (with Raymond Merena) of Bowers and Merena Galleries, Inc., one of America's leading rare coin dealerships, has been involved in the hobby for many years. He served as president of the Professional Numismatists Guild 1977-1979 and is a recipient of the PNG's highest honor, the Founder's Award. A life member (No. 336) of the American Numismatic Association, he became a member of that organization's Board of Governors in 1979, served as vice-president for the 1981-1983 term and as president for the 1983-1985 term. His column, "Numismatic Depth Study," has appeared in *Coin World* for many years and has earned several "Best Columnist Awards" given by the Numismatic Literary Guild. Another column, "Coins and Collectors," appears monthly in *The Numismatist*. His by-line has appeared in all other major numismatic publications, including *Numismatic News*, *Coins Magazine*, and *CoinAge*. He has written the numismatic section of *Encyclopedia Americana*. The author of over two dozen books and several thousand articles, his writing has appeared in such diverse publications as *American Heritage*, *Reader's Digest*, and *Barron's*. In 1976 he received the Alumni Achievement Award from the College of Business Administration, The Pennsylvania State University, from which he graduated earlier.

An Introduction to Collecting by Design Types

Some Background

Collecting coins by design types is a fascinating numismatic pursuit. By this method, instead of collecting a single series or specialty by die varieties or mintmarks, a display is formed consisting of one each of many different motifs. Thus, while the specialist in nickel three-cent pieces desires one of each date and variety from the first year of issue, 1865, to the last, 1889—a collection involving over two dozen pieces—the type set collector is satisfied with just *one* to illustrate the design in his set. It may be the first year of issue, 1865, or it may be an interesting variety such as the 1887/6 overdate, or it may be a rarity in the series—the 1877, for example. But, whatever piece is selected, just one is needed to illustrate the type.

When I first began my professional numismatic activities in the 1950s, collecting by design types was not particularly popular. To be sure, Wayte Raymond had his "National" album pages on the market—pages which included a type set collection. However, by and large the average collector of the day was concerned with putting together a string of dates and mintmarks.

In that long-ago era, when prices for most coins were but a tiny fraction of what they are today, it was indeed possible to collect Indian and Lincoln cents, nickels from the Shield type through the Liberty and Buffalo styles to the Jefferson era, Barber and Mercury dimes, quarters of the Barber, Standing Liberty, and Washington designs, half dollars from the Barber type of the 1890s to date, and other series. A prized rarity such as a 1909-S V.D.B. cent, a piece which is certainly among the most famous of all American coins, was apt to cost all of $20 in Uncirculated preservation. The prized 1856 Flying Eagle cent, also a rarity, was a bit more expensive, but $300 would take home a nice Proof example.

Uncirculated Barber half dollars of the 1892-1915 era cost $5 or so

11

The MCMVII (1907) High Relief $20 gold piece is considered by many to be the most beautiful design type of any issue released in general circulation. The work of noted sculptor Augustus Saint-Gaudens, the motif was created at the personal request of President Theodore Roosevelt. Problems developed in striking the pieces up properly, so after just 11,250 were made, the design was modified to a shallow relief format.

for a common date, while $10 to $12 would buy a beautiful Proof. In those times, $10,000 to $20,000 could buy a truly remarkable and quite comprehensive collection of United States coins, while even the grandest holdings were not apt to be worth in excess of $100,000. If you had told me in 1953 that a quarter century later, in the 1979-1981 era, I would be selling the Garrett Collection for The Johns Hopkins University, and the collection would cross the auction block at $25 million, I would have dismissed the thought as the wildest fiction!

Throughout the 1950s, interest in coins intensified. Proof sets, which could be ordered directly from the Mint for $2.10 each, became a popular investment, and anyone who ordered sets earlier in the decade saw his money multiply several times over, a situation which did not go unnoticed to latecomers—with the result that by 1957 over one million sets were ordered, an all-time record. Investment interest spread to other areas as well. Particularly popular were bank-wrapped rolls of cents, nickels, dimes and quarters dating back to the 1930s. Morgan silver dollars, which were to become popular in a later era, were not in the mainstream of numismatics. Few people collected them.

Investment was not a new word to the hobby. Indeed, the pages of the *American Journal of Numismatics* and other 19th century periodicals are sprinkled with comments concerning investment and speculation. Then, as in later decades, coin sets and series went through phases of popularity and market interest, with the result that prices rose and fell. However, the trend line was upward.

In 1912, Wayte Raymond advertised in *The Numismatist*, official journal of the American Numismatic Association, stating that investment was a normal and desirable aspect of the pursuit of rare coins:

"COINS AS AN INVESTMENT. Many harsh words are said about the collectors who interest themselves in a natural speculation as to whether or not the coins they are buying today will appreciate in value ten years from now. Numismatists of the old school tell us that the true collector is not interested in any such appreciation in the value of his collection but derives his entire profit and pleasure from the coins while in his hands. We feel, however, that the average American collector while he greatly enjoys his coins also feels very pleased if on disposing of his collection he realizes a profit..."

The coin market continued to expand in the 1920s and 1930s, with the 1930s in particular being a period of great growth, a fire fanned by the flames of the commemorative boom of 1935-1936, the introduction of Wayte Raymond's *Standard Catalogue of United States Coins*, the advent of the popular Whitman "penny boards," and the initiation of the *Numismatic Scrapbook Magazine*. The 1940s saw further growth, spurred by postwar inflation and the advent in 1946 of *A Guide Book of United States Coins*, a publication which would go on to be one

The Liberty Walking half dollar, produced from 1916 through 1947, is a favorite with numismatists today. Shown above is one of the scarcer issues toward the end of the coinage span: a 1938-D Adolph A. Weinman, designer of the coin, also produced the Liberty Head or '' Mercury'' dime introduced in 1916.

of the ten best-selling books ever produced.

Still, by the late 1950s, the field of numismatics was limited primarily to aficionados, those who for the most part took the subject seriously and were apt to spend some time each month reading the *Numismatic Scrapbook Magazine, The Numismatist,* or a newspaper-style periodical which made its debut in 1952: *Numismatic News.* Coin clubs flourished, and a nice way to spend a Tuesday evening was to go down to the local Elks Lodge and meet with a couple dozen others who traded coins and exchanged stories.

In the meantime, prices continued their upward trend. Each yearly issue of *A Guide Book of United States Coins* seemed to contain prices higher than the previous one, sometimes sharply higher. Then in 1960 the floodgates opened. Coin collecting became a national pastime. *Coin World* was launched by an Ohio newspaper publisher, and within a few years its circulation surpassed the 150,000 mark! The Philadelphia and Denver mints in 1960 each produced two varieties of Lincoln cents, a Small Date issue and a Large Date issue. It so happened that the 1960 Philadelphia Small Date coin was considered scarce, even rare, at least in the context of other Lincoln cents of the era. Within a few weeks of the discovery of the variety, a $50 bank bag of Philadelphia Small Date cents became worth over $10,000! Here was a chanced to make a fortune. *Time* magazine picked up the news, as did newspapers all across the country. Soon, thousands of newcomers entered the field. While they may have started by buying or finding a 1960 Small Date cent, they went on to discover Liberty Head nickels, $20 gold pieces, and other numismatic delights.

Prices multiplied and then multiplied again. By 1963, prices of a decade earlier, 1953, seemed to be incredible bargains. For example, an Uncirculated 1874 dime worth $9 in 1953, according to *A Guide Book of United States Coins,* was worth $70 a decade later! A Proof 1942 half dollar, worth $3.50 in 1953, went to $23 in the next 10 years, while the rare 1848 quarter eagle with CAL. counterstamped on the reverse, a piece in Uncirculated condition, went from $275 in 1953 to a mind-boggling $5,000 in 1963!

This record of investment success spurred even more interest, and many entered the field of numismatics with investment in mind. They were to be proven right, and just as 1953 prices seemed incredibly low by the hindsight of 1963, by the late 1980s, the prices of 1963 seemed to be incredibly, unbelievably cheap.

By the early 1960s, prices had risen to a point at which $20,000 would no longer build a fairly comprehensive collection of just about everything from Indian cents through Franklin half dollars in Uncirculated or Proof condition. The increased number of collectors caused the supply of coins to be spread widely and caused prices to rise. As a dealer, the change was particularly evident to me. In the 1950s, a client was apt to have a want list stating, for example, that he had all of the Barber quarter dollars by date and mintmark varieties, except for 1896-S, 1901-S, and 1913-S; that in the Barber half dollar series he needed just the mintmark varieties of 1896 and 1897 plus the 1901-S; and that all he needed to fill out his set of Uncirculated Liberty Walking halves was a decent 1921-S. By a decade later, 1963, few people were collecting Barber coins by date and mint varieties. Even Indian cents, which in 1953 were one of the most popular collecting disciplines ever, were fading in popularity. Rather, the typical numismatist settled down to collect just two or three series. He might pick Mercury dimes, Standing Liberty quarters, or Washington quarters, and, even so, it would cost more money to complete these series than it would to have completed a far larger collection ten years earlier.

Realizing that it was no longer feasible for the average person to collect one of everything, in my advertisements I began telling of the virtues of collecting by designs. Around the same time, the Coin & Currency Institute, managed by Robert Friedberg, put on the market its Library of Coins albums, which included albums for collecting by design types. Soon, the Library of Coins albums, which were packaged in book form (unlike the looseleaf binder and separate page format of the earlier Raymond "National" pages), achieved a comfortable niche in the marketplace. Collecting by design types, once the province of relatively few collectors, came to the forefront. Coins which were not great rarities in absolute terms, but which were desirable for inclusion in type sets, were bathed in an intense spotlight. An excellent example is the 1796 quarter dollar, the first year of issue of that denomination. As quarter dollars go, the 1796 is not a fantastic rarity. There are at least several hundred of them in numismatic circulation, of which quite a few dozen can be called Uncirculated. Considerably rarer are high-grade examples of such quarter dollars as 1849-O, 1870-CC, 1871-CC, and 1872-CC. However, only the specialist in quarter dollars by date and mintmark desires these mintmark varieties. On the other hand, anyone aspiring to collect a complete set of United States coins by design type must have a 1796 quarter, for it was the only year in which the Draped Bust obverse design was produced in combination with the Small Eagle reverse. The demand is thus double. The relatively few specialists in quarter dollars by date sequence need a 1796, but a far greater market is represented by collectors aspiring to own a 1796 for a type set collection.

Among gold coins the situation of the 1808 quarter eagle is somewhat similar. This is the only year that its particular design was produced. So, anyone wanting a complete type set of United States gold coins must buy an 1808 to illustrate the Capped Bust to Left variety on a large-size planchet. Thus, a great demand is placed upon the relatively small supply. On the other hand, the Coronet or Liberty Head type quarter eagle was minted from 1840 through 1907, so the type set collector has his pick of many dozens of different varieties, some of which are relatively common.

Building a Type Set

Type sets, like cats, come in many different varieties. There is no such thing as an "official" type set or "standard" type set. One numismatist may desire to collect one each of the different design types produced of copper, nickel, and silver coins of the 20th century, while another may desire to include gold coins as well. Still another numismatist may reach back into the last century and collect designs from 1850 to date. Another collector may go all the way and start with the first federal coinage produced at the Philadelphia Mint in 1793, and continue forward from that point. Still another possibility is to collect by metals—a type set of gold coins, or a type set of copper coins.

Basically, a type set consists of one example of each major design. For example, among small-diameter American one-cent pieces, there are 10 major designs from the first issue of 1856 to the present day. They are:

1. The Flying Eagle cent produced in pattern form in 1856 and in quantity for circulation in 1857 and 1858.

2. The 1859 Indian Cent, bearing on the obverse an Indian motif and on the reverse an laurel wreath. The laurel wreath motif was used only this one year.

3. The 1860-1864 Indian cent struck in copper-nickel alloy, similar to the 1859 Indian cent but with a new reverse design embodying an oak wreath.

4. The Indian cent style from 1864 to 1909 struck on a thin bronze planchet.

5. The first Lincoln cent design produced in 1909 and bearing on the reverse the initials V.D.B., for the engraver, Victor David Brenner.

6. The Lincoln cent style produced from late 1909 through 1958, with the reverse similar to the preceding but without the V.D.B.

7. The 1943 Lincoln cent produced in zinc-coated steel.

8. The Lincoln cent style of 1944 through 1946, produced from melted cartridge cases and of a slightly different alloy.

9. Lincoln cents of the 1959-1982 years, struck in bronze, with the Lincoln Memorial reverse style.

10. Lincoln cents from 1982 to date, Lincoln Memorial reverse, produced from copper-coated zinc.

The preceding list can be modified. For example, among the fourth type of cent, the Indian cent struck on a thin bronze planchet from 1864 through 1909, there are some sub-varieties. Some 1864 issues lack the initial L on the ribbon of the headdress of the Indian and can be considered a separate minor type. Later, in 1886, the obverse was changed slightly, so that on Indian cents from early years through 1886 the last feather of the headdress points between the I and C of AMERICA, whereas certain later 1886 cents and all others through 1909 have the same feather pointing between the C and the A. So, in this illustration, instead of having one variety of Indian cent to illustrate the 1864-1909 thin bronze planchet style, one could have three pieces as follows: 1864 without L on ribbon, 1864 through 1886 with L on ribbon but with last feather of the headdress pointing between the I and C of AMERICA, and the variety from 1886 through 1909 with L on ribbon and with the last feather of the headdress pointing between the C and the A.

Conversely, one could simplify my suggested list of 10 major varieties. You can take the position that the eighth item in my list, the Lincoln cent variety made of a slightly different alloy from 1944 through 1946, is not all that significant, and that it would not have to be included, for it is of the same design as all other cents of the 1909-1958 era (No. 6 in the preceding list).

The point of this is that building a type set is a personal endeavor. You can customize a type set as you wish.

While most numismatists seek to include *any* example of a design type, others have set different requirements. Occasionally a client will aspire to include the first year of issue in each instance. By this method, the nickel three-cent piece in the set would be represented by the first year of issue, 1865, the Liberty Walking half dollar would be represented by the first year of issue, 1916, the Morgan silver dollar would be represented by 1878, and so on.

One memorable client decided to include a major rarity to illustrate the type, certainly not the best way to collect economically, but he had elegant taste and a checkbook balance to match. Thus, to illustrate the Shield nickel style of 1867 through 1883, without rays on the reverse, he picked not a relatively common issue such as an 1882 or 1883, but, rather, the scarcest variety in that span, the highly-prized 1877. To illustrate the Mercury dime series from 1916 through 1945 he picked—you guessed it—an Uncirculated 1916-D! The result was a type set worth a king's ransom, or at least that of a prince—and one which attracted attention wherever it was displayed.

Still another acquaintance put together a set of different design types of coins produced only at the Denver Mint. Another numismatist did the same thing for Carson City. Still another endeavored

In 1883 a new type of nickel five-cent piece appeared, the Liberty Head style, modeled, it was said, after the goddess Diana. This classical motif continued in use for circulating coinage through 1912. The very first 1883 issues omitted the word CENTS on the reverse—the style shown above. This error was recognized, and the reverse was subsequently redesigned.

to include the *last* year of issue of each design, an interesting coun-
terfoil to the more common practice of including the first.

What grades should I buy? The answer to this admits many different possibilities. In general, the prices of modern coins are such that
designs from 1950 to date can be readily obtained in Uncirculated
and Proof state. Issues of the early 20th century can be collected in
grades from Extremely Fine upward, depending upon how much
you want to pay. The same goes for pieces minted in the late 19th
century. Coins produced from 1793 through about 1840 are typically
collected in higher circulated grades, Fine to Extremely Fine or AU.
A nice Extremely Fine or AU piece has the advantage that it displays
all of the design detail, nearly all of the sharpness, and is almost
as appealing as an Uncirculated piece, but in the marketplace it is
apt to cost just a tiny fraction of the price of a higher condition coin.
Again, one's checkbook balance is a factor. However, even if you could
afford it, it is exceedingly unlikely that a complete type set of United States coins in Choice Uncirculated grade could be put together
in your lifetime. No matter how much money you had at your dis-
posal, you might be stymied when it comes to obtaining superb
pieces of certain early types.

Probably the best way to begin a type set of United States coins
is to start with issues of the 20th century. By doing this, you can
gain a feeling and appreciation for the subject, you can study and
read about many different pieces, and you will then gain the knowl-
edge to be able to better choose coins from an earlier era, if you later
decide to expand. At the start, I suggest acquiring 20th century pieces
in the various alloys of copper, nickel, and silver. From that point,
you can expand to 19th century pieces or, you can increase the
breadth of your collection by adding gold.

As a point of information, technically the 20th century started on
January 1, 1901. The year 1900 was the last year of the 19th century.
In practice, most numismatists overlook this distinction, and if you
show someone a 1900 half dollar, they will probably tell you it is a
"20th century coin." Similarly, when the year 1900 arrived on the
American scene, celebrations were held for the "new century." I have
every expectation that when the year 2000 rolls around there will
be a lot of merrymaking all over the world—few people will want
to wait for the proper year, which is 2001.

A Logical Way to Collect

In 1985, Tom Becker, who has long maintained his post as the senior
numismatist at Bowers and Merena Galleries, Ray Merena, and I were
discussing the popularity by collecting by design types. One of the
obstacles placed in the way of collectors, we determined, was the

lack of availability of holders which permitted one to asser
States coins by design types in a *logical* fashion. After c
thinking and planning, we came up with what was ever
as the "Kingswood Series" of custom-made, gold-imprii
which made its debut later in the same year. Following the initiai
announcement, Tom was overwhelmed with orders, and it was several months until he could catch up! None of us had any idea the demand would be so great.

The present text is not intended to be a sales presentation for the
"Kingswood Series" holders for these holders have literally sold
themselves. Rather, it is to illustrate what I consider to be a logical
way to collect a type set. You may disagree and may want to take
advantage of any one of the other fine holder formats available in
the market, or you may want to keep your coins in individual holders,
in plastic envelopes, or some other way. This, of course, is up to you.
However, as the "Kingswood Series" concept has proved so popular and, as noted, seems to be quite logical in its inception, I discuss
it here.

The "Kingswood Series" holders trace the progress of coin designs
as they actually appeared on the American scene. For example, the earliest holder in the series, designated as KW-1, contains design types
of United States coins *introduced* during the 1793-1799 years. The
Draped Bust large cent, for example, first made its appearance in
1796 but was continued through 1807. Thus, this type is found in
holder KW-1, which covers *new issues* from 1793 to 1799 inclusive.
There is no opening for the Draped Bust large cent in the second
holder, KW-2, for the second holder covers the 1800-1830 time span,
by which time the Draped Bust cent was already a familiar design.
However, the opening for the Draped Bust cent in the KW-1 holder
notes that the design was produced from 1796 through 1807. To reiter-
ate, in the "Kingswood Series" holders each design type appears
in the holder covering the year in which it was *introduced*. To my way
of thinking, this is more meaningful than including the coin twice
or putting it in a later holder.

By means of the "Kingswood Series" holders, one can acquire a
series of holders covering different time spans. Each holder is a complete display on its own and can stand all by itself.

One of the prime advantages of building a type set is that you will
become acquainted with many different series covering a wide variety of designs and eras. Each coin is different, each has its own story to tell—and often the stories are fascinating. While the following
text describes and illustrates major designs in the American series,
I recommend that you go beyond what I have noted and study in
detail any designs that are particularly fascinating to you. For example, the $10 and $20 coinage of Augustus Saint-Gaudens could form

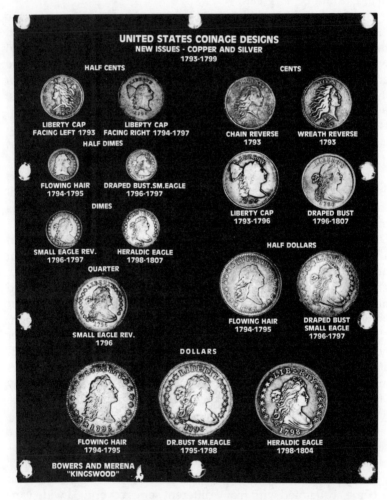

UNITED STATES COINAGE DESIGNS
NEW ISSUES - COPPER AND SILVER
1793-1799

HALF CENTS

LIBERTY CAP
FACING LEFT 1793

LIBERTY CAP
FACING RIGHT 1794-1797

HALF DIMES

FLOWING HAIR
1794-1795

DRAPED BUST.SM.EAGLE
1796-1797

DIMES

SMALL EAGLE REV.
1796-1797

HERALDIC EAGLE
1798-1807

QUARTER

SMALL EAGLE REV.
1796

CENTS

CHAIN REVERSE
1793

WREATH REVERSE
1793

LIBERTY CAP
1793-1796

DRAPED BUST
1796-1807

HALF DOLLARS

FLOWING HAIR
1794-1795

DRAPED BUST
SMALL EAGLE
1796-1797

DOLLARS

FLOWING HAIR
1794-1795

DR.BUST SM.EAGLE
1795-1798

HERALDIC EAGLE
1798-1804

BOWERS AND MERENA
"KINGSWOOD"

A "Kingswood" plastic display holder for United States coinage designs, new copper and silver issues introduced during the 1793-1799 years, times of growth and experimentation at the new Philadelphia Mint. In addition to the "Kingswood" style holder shown above, a number of other desirable brands and configurations are available in the marketplace.

A "Kingswood" holder for new copper and silver coin designs introduced during the 1800-1830 span. No great rarities are featured, but the half dime type of 1800-1805 is quite scarce.

a fascinating chapter in itself. Similarly, the Morgan silver dollar, certainly one of the most popular of all coins in numismatics today, could form the subject of a detailed book—as indeed it has on several occasions. It could be that the acquisition of a particular coin for your type set will open the gate to forming a specialized variety collection of a given series. Few collectors endeavor over a period of time to acquire just one set. A number of numismatists who have beautiful type sets also have specialized collections of certain series, such as a set of Mercury dimes, a collection of 1793-1857 large cents by die varieties, a date collection of Liberty Walking half dollars, or another area of interest.

A good magnifying glass of medium power is your passport to many discoveries, and in connection with assembling a set I strongly recommend that you spend at least several minutes—if not longer—studying each coin. Observe the lettering, the motifs on the obverse and reverse, how the designs were made, and anything else that crosses your field of vision. Then, with the coin in your hand or nearby, read about it. You will find that 1 plus 1, rather than equaling 2, may equal 3 or 4. That is, owning a coin provides some degree of satisfaction, and reading about a coin also provides a degree of satisfaction, but the combination of owning a piece and reading about it at the same time provides a much greater combined degree of pleasure!

Additional Notes

The following pages outline United States coins by design types. Each issue is illustrated, its technical aspects are given, and a discussion of it then follows. The designers of various early issues, particularly coins of the years from 1793 through the 1830s, are identified based upon research done by Don Taxay, Walter Breen, Robert W. Julian and others. In some instances, the attributions are so-called "educated guesses," for during the very early stages of the Philadelphia Mint's operation, few records were kept on design and artistic matters.

The diameters given for various pieces are fairly standard after the introduction of steam-powered coinage presses (beginning at the Philadelphia Mint in 1836), but among earlier pieces there are many variations. Thus, among 1793-1796 large cents of the Liberty Cap motif, for example, there may be a difference of a millimeter or two or three among examples actually measured. Similarly, dimes of the late 1820s and early 1830s vary in diameter from issue to issue. Other examples could be cited.

The mintage figures given are taken from various sources listed in the bibliography of the present book. In some instances, particularly among earlier pieces, such figures are estimates. And, in even more instances, there is a strong possibility that the mintage figures for a given year or type do not necessarily represent pieces exclusively dated within the time span indicated. For example, the gold quarter eagle of 1808 is listed as having a mintage of 2,710 pieces, based upon figures kept by the Mint at the time. However, during the early years the Mint kept figures on a *fiscal* year basis, running from the summer of one year to the summer of another year, rather than on a *calendar* year basis. Further, it was the practice to keep earlier-dated dies on hand until they broke, wore out, or until a *major* change was made in the design. Thus it is entirely possible that the 2,710 quarter eagles believed to have been minted with the 1808 date may represent some pieces dated earlier and produced from leftover dies.

On the other hand, the mintage figure of 6,146 pieces coined of the 1796 quarter dollar is probably accurate, for this represents the first year of issue—so no earlier pieces could be included in that figure. No other quarter dollar dies were made until 1804, thus the year 1796, representing a distinct design type, is isolated in time.

Mintage figures given for Proof coins represent the number of pieces *struck*, which may differ from the number of pieces actually *distributed*. For example, it is known that among Proof gold coins of the 1860-1900 years, many pieces were unsold and were later melted or placed into circulation. Thus, such Proofs are considerably rarer than the mintage figures indicate. In other instances, mintage figures seem to be grossly erroneous. For example, it is reported that 682 Matte Proof specimens were struck of the 1910 quarter eagle, a figure which is over double that of any other Proof quarter eagle and over triple that of most others of the 1908-1915 span. And yet, surveys of auction appearances and private transactions show that 1910 quarter eagles do not appear significantly more often than other quarter eagles of the era—such as 1908 (236 Proofs reported minted), 1909 (139 Proofs), or 1911 (191 Proofs).

Proof sets were first sold to the public in 1858, during which year approximately 80 silver sets and a substantially larger number of individual copper-nickel Flying Eagle cents were produced. Proof mintage figures for silver and gold coins are published in *A Guide Book of United States Coins* and elsewhere for most issues from 1858 onward. However, Proof mintages of smaller denominations—cents, two-cent pieces, nickel three-cent pieces and nickel five-cent pieces—are guesswork prior to about 1878. Complicating the situation is the fact that restrikes were made of certain Proof issues, particularly early key dates (such as the 1858 Liberty Seated dollar). And, for Proofs of all types minted *before* 1858, the quantities produced can only be estimated.

Thus, the disparity in certain instances between a high number of Proofs produced and a lower number of Proofs actually distributed (such as among 1860-1900 gold coins, as earlier noted), the occasional situation of restriking, the lack of precise Proof mintage figures for certain coinage areas, and the inaccuracy of other figures (such as the previously-mentioned 1910 quarter eagle) result in the compilation of Proof totals being an estimate or approximation. The totals are valuable, however, in a relative sense. In general, a type coin struck in the same metal, and from the same historical era, is available in Proof grade in proportion to the mintage figures; that is, a design of which just 1,500 Proofs were minted is about three times rarer than a contemporary type of which 4,500 Proofs were struck.

Proofs, having been made especially for collectors, were sold at a premium and were for the most part preserved over the years. Although many have fallen victim to mishandling, loss, spending for face value, and, in particular, cleaning, still most Proofs survive today. Although no certain determination can ever be made, it is probably accurate to say that, for example, of Proof silver coins minted during the 1860-1870 decade, perhaps 50 or 60% survive today, and of this percentage possibly 10% to 20% exist in relatively unimpaired condition. As we go forward in time, the survival rate increases. Of Proof silver coins minted during the 1900-1910 decade, probably 60 to 70 percent survive, including perhaps 15% to 25% in unimpaired condition. Moving ahead to the 1950-1960 decade, probably 90% or more of all Proof coins minted during that time still survive, with 50% or more being unimpaired. Among Proof coins of the past few years, nearly all survive as issued.

On the other hand, the survival of early Uncirculated or business strike pieces is a matter of chance. From the 1930s onward, most new issues were saved in quantities by collectors, dealers, and speculators, so with relatively few exceptions (such as the 1936-D quarter), examples are relatively easily acquired. Among earlier pieces the situation is far different. The only pre-1900 regular issue United States coins readily available in Uncirculated grades are Morgan silver dollars of many different dates—due to the Treasury policy of hoarding them at the time of issue—and the 1883 without CENTS Liberty head nickel, for the latter issue was hoarded by the public because of the Mint's mistake in the design.

There are numerous 19th century coins which are readily available in circulated grades such as Fine through AU but which are great rarities in superb Uncirculated state. Examples abound, particularly in the field of gold coins. Try, for example, to obtain a superb Uncirculated $20 double eagle of the 1850-1866 era, or of the second type in the double eagle series, the style minted from 1866 through 1876, and the search may take many *years*. Or, try to locate a superb Uncirculated Liberty Seated silver dollar of the 1840-1865 style. It won't be easy. For many 19th century type coins, Proofs are far more available than are top-echelon Uncirculated coins.

Dr. William H. Sheldon, in his *Penny Whimsy* book on 1793-1814 large cents, stated that the completion of a set of large cents in perfect or MS-70 grade was impossible, which, of course, it is. He likened the situation to a golfer expecting to make the round of 18 holes in just 18 strokes. *Theoretically* it could happen, but *practically* no one has come even remotely close to doing it. So it is with forming a type set of United States coins. Among the early issues, perfection or near perfection is not possible. Even Extremely Fine and AU examples are elusive for many design types. This, perhaps, is precisely as it should be—for it wouldn't be much fun if one could simply write out a check and acquire in one fell swoop a complete type set of United States coins from 1793 to date, in Uncirculated or Proof grade. Going back to Dr. Sheldon's golfing example, if pursuers of that sport routinely went around the course in 18 strokes, interest would have died long ago—and golf would no longer be popular. In coins, as in other pursuits, the thrill of the chase is a large part of the enjoyment derived. Whereas a type set of coin designs from recent decades can be completed in relatively short notice, a top-grade Uncirculated and Proof type set of American coin designs of the early part of the present century will be a challenge and may require many months of looking, even if one has the money to instantly buy any coin wanted. A completion of earlier areas of your type set will likewise be a challenge, with the length of time for completion being dependent upon the grade objectives selected. No matter what grades are picked, even low grades for some of the rarities, it will take a long time to find coins with attractive surfaces, pleasing overall appearance, and other characteristics which make each item "just right" for your display.

I recommend that in addition to acquiring coins for your type set and reading *numismatic* books of interest (the bibliography gives some suggestions in this regard), you seek out some general American history books. When I see a 1906 Barber half dollar, for example, I can also conjure in my mind a vision of America at that time—the novelty of the automobile, the omnipresence of horses and horse-drawn vehicles on the American scene, the beginnings of the airplane, Theodore Roosevelt in the White House, and many more things. Similarly, a coin of 1864 can evoke thoughts of the Civil War, the conflict between the North and the South, thoughts of Jefferson Davis and Abraham Lincoln, and so on. Coins are the footprints of history, it has been said, and to study coins alone—without appreciating their history—is to get just part of the picture.

Read the following text, go beyond this book to investigate numismatically any particular design types that pique your interest, and then relate these pieces to contemporary American history. Do these things, and a glorious collecting experience awaits you! And, more good news: in the past, a carefully-formed type set, gathered over a period of years and held as a long-term investment, has typically outperformed just about any other investment medium you care to name. History has a way of repeating itself, and in numismatics, today's market price has a way of being tomorrow's bargain. While the future is unknown, the outlook seems favorable that coins will continue their excellent investment record. There you have it: a fascinating collecting pursuit combined with what may be an excellent investment potential. Multiple pleasures await you!

Chapter 2

New Issues
COPPER AND SILVER 1793-1799

The years from 1793 through 1799 saw the advent of 16 different design types among copper and silver denominations. Included in a type set containing these are some of the most desirable and rare examples of our nation's numismatic heritage.

After much deliberation and several false starts, the government acquired buildings in Philadelphia in 1792 and set about establishing a native mint. Toward the end of the year, patterns were produced of several types, including the 1792 Silver Center cent, the curious and rare Birch cent, the silver half *disme* (believed to have been struck off the premises in a nearby location, for the Mint facilities were not quite ready), the *disme,* and the enigmatic eagle-on-globe piece, believed to be either a cent or a quarter.

The following year, 1793, marked the appearance of the first circulating coins produced in large numbers, the half cent and three major types of large cents. At the outset, only copper coins were produced, for certain mint officials had not been able to meet the monetary surety or bond required before precious metal production could ensue. This difficulty was overcome, and in 1794 the first silver denominations, consisting of the half dime, half dollar, and dollar, were produced, to be followed in 1796 by the dime and quarter.

A copper and silver type set of this era includes a number of major scarcities and rarities. Notable among them are the 1793 half cent, a coin rare in all grades, the famous 1793 Chain and Wreath cents, the 1796 quarter, and, in particular, the 1796-1797 style half dollar. Each one of these is quite important in its own right.

During the 1793-1799 years there was virtually no interest in numismatics in America. As a result, new specimens of the coinage were not set aside as they were issued. The survival of higher grade pieces is thus a matter of chance. In the early 1960s, numismatists were startled when the estate of Lord St. Oswald crossed the auction block in London. It seems that this otherwise forgotten English gentleman

The Liberty Cap motif was used on cents from 1793-1796 (the variety shown above is Sheldon No. 22 of 1794). The same motif, with Miss Liberty facing to the right, was used on half cents from 1794 through 1797. All dies of the era were finished by hand, with the result that numerous interesting variations can be studied and collected today.

The Draped Bust motif, shown above on a large cent of 1798, was a popular motif across the copper and silver coinage spectrum. The portrait is said to have been suggested by artist Gilbert Stuart and first appeared on certain varieties of 1795 silver dollars.

The Flowing Hair motif, as employed on the 1795 silver dollar shown above, was a popular design and was used on half dimes, half dollars, and dollars of the 1794-1795 years. The reverse displays the so-called "Small Eagle."

visited the United States in 1795 and stopped by at the Philadelphia Mint, securing specimens of cents, half dollars, dollars, and other pieces as souvenirs. Included in the treasure trove dispersed at auction were two Uncirculated 1794 dollars, believed to be the finest surviving examples.

Occasionally examples of 1796 and 1797 cents in Uncirculated grade are encountered, perhaps remnants from the so-called Nichols Hoard, discussed at length in Dr. William H. Sheldon's *Penny Whimsy* book. Typically, these have glossy brown or reddish-brown surfaces and are quite attractive. A number of 1796 quarter dollars in Uncirculated condition, many with prooflike surfaces, still exist. In the early 1940s, Abe Kosoff reported viewing many dozens of these, pieces owned by James G. Macallister, an old-time Philadelphia dealer. Where these went, no one knows, and it is doubtful if many of the pieces in the hoard can be tracked down today.

Several designs recur among coins of the 1793 to 1799 years. The 1793 Chain and Wreath cent designs are distinctive and were not used on other denominations, but the head of Miss Liberty with a Liberty Cap behind was used on the half cent of 1793 and, facing in the opposite direction (right instead of left), on large cents from 1793 through 1796. The Liberty Cap motif, the symbol of freedom derived from the cap given to slaves freed in ancient times, occurs over a long period in American numismatics, particularly as part of the Liberty Seated design used on silver coinage of the 1837-1891 span. Interestingly, Frank Gasparro, chief engraver of the Philadelphia Mint, proposed a revival of the Liberty Cap design, quite similar to that used on early cents and half cents, when Congress proposed issuing a new metallic dollar in the late 1970s. However, the pressure of special interests prevailed, and the liberty cap design was not to be. Instead, the Susan B. Anthony dollar was created. The more things change, the more they are the same, it has been said, and numerous other instances can be cited of early designs or motifs being resurrected in later years. The Heraldic Eagle design, used on silver dollars beginning in 1798, was also used, in modified form, as the reverse of the Kennedy half dollar, which was first produced in 1964. Actually, the Heraldic Eagle motif is simply an adaptation of the Great Seal of the United States.

Half dimes, half dollars, and silver dollars of 1794 and 1795 are found with the so-called Flowing Hair motif. Each features an attractively styled head of Miss Liberty facing to the right, flowing tresses behind, with the word LIBERTY above, stars to the left and right, and the date below.

The Draped Bust design, said to have been modeled from a sketch by artist Gilbert Stuart, is found on coinage beginning with the silver dollar of 1795, expanding to the cent, half dime, dime, quarter,

The Heraldic Eagle motif was used on various silver and gold coins during the turn of the 19th century, with the 1799/8 overdate silver dollar shown above being but one of many pieces employing the style, which was an adaptation of the Great Seal of the United States.

and half dollar of 1796. Curiously, the motif was not used on the half cent until later, in 1800.

The wreath was employed as part of the reverse design of most coinage of the 1793-1799 years, with the 1793 Chain reverse cent being a notable exception. Half cents and large cents have the denomination within the wreath and UNITED STATES OF AMERICA around the outside border, while the silver denominations have an eagle at the center. Early versions are designated as the Small Eagle design and feature a bird with thin wings perched on a cloud. This was followed by the Heraldic Eagle motif, which was an adaptation of the Great Seal of the United States, as noted.

The edges of half cents from 1793 through part of 1795 are lettered TWO HUNDRED FOR A DOLLAR, a feature intended to furnish useful information and also to deter clipping or edge filing. Many Liberty Cap cents of the era have edge lettering, as do all half dollars and silver dollars. The half dime, dime, and quarter were deemed to be too thin for edge lettering to be placed on the coin or to be read properly.

During the cradle days of the Philadelphia Mint, the 1793 through 1799 years discussed here, relatively few coins were produced in comparison to the number of pieces needed for circulation. So, the channels of commerce were filled with coins struck elsewhere. British copper coins were in abundance, as were numerous coppers produced by Connecticut, New Jersey, Vermont, Massachusetts, and other entities. Silver coins were apt to be Spanish-American types, the silver-dollar size eight-real pieces of Mexico and southward, and their fractional parts such as the four reales, two reales, and one real. These fractional pieces were referred to as "bits." Hence, a two-real coin, equal in value to a quarter dollar, was familiarly known as "two bits," a term which still survives in the English language. It was not until 1857 that Congress felt that enough United States coins had been produced that foreign coins should no longer be legal tender. If you were to have entered a tavern in the year 1796, for example, the chances are that a handful of pocket change, upon inspection, would have contained very few Philadelphia Mint coins. It took a decade or two until enough pieces were in circulation that they were encountered in everyday transactions.

HALF CENT
1793 Liberty Cap Facing Left

Designed by: Adam Eckfeldt (?)
Issue Date: 1793
Composition: Copper
Diameter: 21.2 to 24.6 mm
Weight: 104 grains
Edge: Lettered TWO HUNDRED FOR A DOLLAR.
Business strike mintage: 35,334
Proof mintage: None

The obverse of the design portrays Miss Liberty, with features engraved in detail, facing to the viewer's left, with a liberty cap on a pole behind her head. The word LIBERTY is above, and the date 1793 is below. A circle of beads is around the outer edge. The reverse consists of a wreath with leaves and berries, open at the top, and tied with a bow below. The denomination HALF CENTS is at the center, while UNITED STATES OF AMERICA and the fraction 1/200 comprises the border. A circle of beads is at the rim. Several die varieties were produced.

1793 half cents were coined in late spring or summer of the year, using a design adapted from the famous Libertas Americana medal issued in France. Walter Breen suggests that Robert Birch and Adam Eckfeldt produced the reverse dies, while Birch cut the obverse. The first delivery of struck pieces is said to have occurred on July 20, 1793.

Typically encountered 1793 half cents are apt to show extensive wear, with Fair, Good and Very Good examples representing the majority. Fine pieces are rare, Very Fine coins are rarer still, and pieces meriting the Extremely Fine or About Uncirculated designation are seldom met with. Occasionally an Uncirculated piece crosses the auction block. Many examples of 1793 half cents in grades from Fair through Fine show the words HALF CENT on the reverse weakly. Only a few hundred 1793 half cents survive today. The coin is scarce in all grades and is considered to be a key issue.

HALF CENT
1794-1797 Liberty Cap Facing Right

Designed by: Robert Scot
Issue Dates: 1794-1797
Composition: Copper
Diameter: 23.5 mm
Weight: 104 grains (thick planchet) 84 grains (thin planchet)
Edge: Lettered TWO HUNDRED FOR A DOLLAR; some plain
Business strike mintage: 359,529
Proof mintage: None

Half cents of the 1794-1797 years depict on the obverse Miss Liberty facing to the viewer's right, with LIBERTY above and the date below. Behind her flowing hair is a liberty cap on a pole. The edge is a series of denticles or indentations; the beaded border of 1793 had been discontinued. The reverse is similar in concept to 1793 except for the denticulated border. Although issues of 1794-1797 are commonly grouped together as a single type, in actuality half cents of 1794 have a larger head of Miss Liberty, while those of 1795 through 1797 have a delicate cameo-like head in a more open field area.

In general, pieces dated 1794 are rare in grades of Extremely Fine or better, while pieces dated 1795 can be acquired in Extremely Fine, About Uncirculated, or even Uncirculated grade, although an Uncirculated specimen may require several years of searching. The half cents of 1794 are apt to have rough surfaces, often with dark color or granularity. On the other hand, smooth, light brown surfaces are characteristic of 1795 through 1797.

All 1794 cents have lettered edges, as do certain 1795 issues and a few minted in 1797. The rest have plain edges.

A popular condition objective for this style is Fine to Very Fine. Such pieces are sharp enough to show the details, yet they are priced much less than higher grades. Good or Very Good pieces, if carefully selected, can be quite attractive and desirable.

CENT
1793 Chain Reverse

Designed by: Henry Voigt
Issue date: 1793
Composition: Copper
Diameter: Average 26 to 27 mm
Weight: 208 grains
Edge: Vine and bars design
Business strike mintage: 36,103
Proof mintage: None

This, the first American cent made for general circulation, depicts on the obverse Miss Liberty facing right, with LIBERTY above and the date 1793 below. The reverse illustrates a link chain motif at the center, enclosing ONE CENT and the fraction 1/100, while at the outer border is UNITED STATES OF AMERI. on the first variety minted (Sheldon die variety No. 1) and UNITED STATES OF AMERICA on others. The border consists of a rim without beads or denticles.

Appearing early in the year, the "Chain cent" evoked unfavorable criticism, with one newspaper report stating that Miss Liberty appeared to be "in a fright" and that the chain motif on the reverse was but a ill omen for a country which had recently secured its freedom (from England). The criticism was heeded, and before long the Chain design was discontinued.

Specimens today are scarce in all grades. The obverse design details were lightly cut into the dies, and the result is that only the highest grade pieces are apt to show well defined strands of Miss Liberty's hair in the central portions. It is often the case that the obverse of a given piece will be a grade or two less than the reverse. Examples are most frequently seen in lower grades, from Fair through Good to Very Good. Fine to Very Fine pieces are elusive, while examples in Extremely Fine or better preservation are very rare.

CENT
1793 Wreath Reverse

Designed by: Adam Eckfeldt
Issue date: 1793
Composition: Copper
Diameter: 26 to 28 mm
Weight: 208 grains
Edge: Vine and bars design, or lettered ONE HUNDRED FOR
    A DOLLAR
Business strike mintage: 63,353
Proof mintage: None

The second major design in the cent series is the so-called Wreath style. The obverse was redesigned from the earlier motif and now features Miss Liberty in higher relief, with the hair details more pronounced, LIBERTY above her head, the date 1793 below, and above the date a sprig or leaf design. The reverse consists of an open wreath tied with a bow at the bottom, enclosing ONE CENT, with UNITED STATES OF AMERICA and the fraction 1/100 surrounding. Both obverse and reverse are protected by a high rim with a bead design between the rim and the field.

The Wreath style is the most often seen variety of 1793, although examples in all grades are scarce. A number of different die varieties were produced, some of which have a vine and bars design on the edge and others of which are lettered ONE HUNDRED FOR A DOLLAR. Examples can be found in all grades, in Fair through Uncirculated, although pieces in Extremely Fine or better preservation are seldom met with. During this period, the Mint acquired copper from many different sources, with the result that the surfaces of early half cents and cents are apt to vary considerably, even on higher grade pieces. More often than not, the fields of a piece show porosity or graininess.

CENT
1793-1796 Liberty Cap

Designed by: John Gardner
Issue dates: 1793-1796
Composition: Copper
Diameter: Average 29 mm
Weight: 208 grains (thick planchet), 168 grains (thin planchet)
Edge: Early pieces lettered ONE HUNDRED FOR A DOLLAR;
** the later pieces have plain edges**
Business strike mintage: 1,577,902
Proof mintage: None

The Liberty Cap motif made its appearance late in 1793 and was continued through 1796. The design was later (1794-1797) used on half cents. The motif features Miss Liberty facing to the right, a liberty cap on pole behind her head, LIBERTY above, and the date below. The reverse displays an open wreath enclosing ONE CENT, with UNITED STATES OF AMERICA and the fraction 1/100 surrounding. 1793 Liberty Cap cents have a beaded border, while those dated from 1794 through 1796 have denticles. The edges of 1793, 1794, and some 1795 pieces are lettered ONE HUNDRED FOR A DOLLAR, while later issues have a plain edge. Dozens of different die varieties were produced of this motif from 1793 through 1796, with the result that there are many possibilities from which the collector can choose. The numismatist seeking simply a design type in grades from Good through Fine can select from pieces of the 1794, 1795, or 1796 dates, for 1793 Liberty Cap cents are much rarer and more expensive. In higher grades, Extremely Fine to Uncirculated, pieces dated 1795 are more readily available than those dated 1794 or 1796, with 1796 cents closely following. The sharpness of strike, planchet quality, and surface characteristics vary widely among cents of this style, so some searching may be needed to find one that is "just right."

Note: See Chapter 12, "Some Interesting Options," for additional information.

CENT
1796-1807 Draped Bust

Designed by: Robert Scot
Issue dates: 1796-1807
Composition: Copper
Diameter: 29 mm
Weight: 168 grains
Edge: Plain
Business strike mintage: 16,111,810
Proof mintage: None

In the cent series the Draped Bust obverse appeared in 1796 (the year after it made its initial appearance in American coinage on the 1795 silver dollar). Patterned after a proposal of artist Gilbert Stuart, and translated into the coinage medium by Robert Scot, the style features Miss Liberty with flowing hair, a ribbon behind her head, and drapery covering her plunging neckline. LIBERTY is above, and the date is below. The reverse is similar to the preceding design and consists of an open wreath enclosing ONE CENT with UNITED STATES OF AMERICA and the fraction 1/100 surrounding. Denticles are around the border, although on some varieties they are not particularly well defined.

Many different die varieties were made within this span. The numismatist seeking something different can find an example from a blundered die, such as with the incorrect fraction 1/000, at little extra cost. Among Draped Bust cents, rare dates are 1799 and 1804. Other issues are seen with frequency. Examples are readily available in all grades from Fair through Extremely Fine, with AU coins being rare and Uncirculated pieces being extremely rare.

HALF DIME
1794-1795 Flowing Hair

Designed by: Robert Scot
Issue dates: 1794-1795
Composition: 0.8924 part silver and 0.1076 part copper
Diameter: 16.5 mm
Weight: 20.8 grains
Edge: Reeded
Business strike mintage: 86,416
Proof mintage: None

The obverse of the 1794-1795 half dime style portrays Miss Liberty with flowing hair, facing right, with LIBERTY above and the date 1795 below. Eight stars are behind her head and seven are in front. The reverse illustrates a delicate or "small" eagle perched on a cloud, within an open wreath, with UNITED STATES OF AMERICA surrounding. Denticles are around the border, as on all half dimes from this design forward. Curiously, neither this half dime design nor the following two motifs bear a designation of denomination or value.

Of the two dates in which Flowing Hair half dimes were made, the 1795 is more often seen than 1794. Specimens of either date are typically encountered in grades from Good through Fine to Very Fine. Extremely Fine examples are elusive, and AU coins are rare. Uncirculated pieces are apt to be encountered only when great collections come on the market. Many pieces are found with a series of parallel lines or adjustment marks, produced at the Mint during the planchet preparation process. In keeping with other pieces of the era, the striking is apt to be inconsistent, and often one area or another will show some normal weakness.

Note: See Chapter 12, "Some Interesting Options," for the 1792 half disme.

HALF DIME
1796-1797 Draped Bust, Small Eagle

Designed by: Robert Scot
Issue dates: 1796-1797
Composition: 0.8924 part silver, 0.1076 part copper
Diameter: 16.5 mm
Weight: 20.8 grains
Edge: Reeded
Business strike mintage: 54,757
Proof mintage: None

The Draped Bust style is believed to have been the work of Robert Scot, who followed the proposal made by artist Gilbert Stuart. The obverse depicts Miss Liberty with flowing hair, a ribbon behind her head, with drapery covering her plunging neckline. LIBERTY is above and the date is below. 1796 half dimes have eight stars to the left and seven to the right on the obverse, while those dated 1797 come in three variations, with a total of 13, 15, or 16 stars. The reverse features an open wreath enclosing a small eagle perched on a cloud, the eagle being smaller in size than that used in 1794-1795, and with the cloud more pronounced and higher above the wreath bow. UNITED STATES OF AMERICA surrounds. Again, there is no indication of value or denomination.

All half dimes of this design type are scarce. Most often encountered are lower grades from About Good through Fine. Very Fine pieces are elusive, Extremely Fine coins are rare and pieces in AU or better preservation are seldom met with. In the 1960s, when James F. Ruddy was gathering photographs for his *Photograde* book, he found that examples of this half dime type were among the most difficult to locate. As is true of other early silver coins, pieces are apt to have mint-caused adjustment marks and to be weakly struck in certain areas, particularly at the center of the eagle on the reverse.

DIME
1796-1797 Draped Bust, Small Eagle

Designed by: Robert Scot
Issues dates: 1796-1797
Composition: 0.8924 part silver, 0.1076 part copper
Diameter: 19 mm
Weight: 41.6 grains
Edge: Reeded
Business strike mintage: 47,396
Proof mintage: None

The design of the 1796-1797 dime parallels that of the contemporary half dime. The obverse depicts Miss Liberty with flowing hair, a ribbon behind her head, and drapery covering her plunging neckline. LIBERTY is above and the date is below. Thirteen obverse stars are to be found on the 1796 dime, while dimes of 1797 come with either 13 or 16 obverse stars. The reverse consists of an open wreath, tied with a bow at the bottom, enclosing a small eagle perched on a cloud, with UNITED STATES OF AMERICA surrounding. No indication of denomination or value appears.

Examples of this type are most often encountered in lower grades from About Good to Fine. Very Fine examples are scarce, Extremely Fine pieces are rare, and coins in higher ranges are very rare. Occasionally an AU or Uncirculated 1796 dime will be found, but few pieces dated 1797 exist in Mint State or close to it. Mint-caused adjustment marks are often seen, as are areas of normal light striking. These pieces were meant strictly for utilitarian use, and no thought was given to producing pieces for collectors.

DIME
1798-1807 Draped Bust, Heraldic Eagle

Designed by: Robert Scot
Issue dates: 1798-1807
Composition: 0.8924 part silver, 0.1076 part copper
Diameter: 19 mm
Weight: 41.6 grains
Edge: Reeded
Business strike mintage: 422,010
Proof mintage: None

The dimes minted from 1798 through 1807 display the Draped Bust obverse as preceding, except that the star count is now standardized at a total of 13, with seven to the left and six to the right. The reverse is new and is designated as the Heraldic Eagle style. Patterned after the Great Seal of the United States, it features an eagle at the center, with a shield on its breast, and a ribbon bearing the inscription E PLURIBUS UNUM in its beak. Above is an arc of clouds, below which are stars. UNITED STATES OF AMERICA surrounds. There is no indication of value or denomination. A number of different die varieties exist within this range, including the overdates 1798/7 and examples with different numbers of stars above the eagle on the reverse.

In keeping with other early silver coins, examples most often seen are in grades from About Good through Fine. Very Fine pieces are somewhat scarce, Extremely Fine coins are scarcer yet, AU examples are rare, and Uncirculated coins are very rare. Many show Mint-caused adjustment marks. Areas of light striking are the rule, not the exception, and nearly all pieces have some flatness of stars or other details, with the lightness of strike generally increasing as the design continued in use; that is, specimens dated toward the end of the series, 1805 and later, are apt to be more lightly struck than those dated 1798.

QUARTER DOLLAR
1796 Draped Bust, Small Eagle

Designed by: Robert Scot
Issue date: 1796
Composition: 0.8924 part silver, 0.1076 part copper
Diameter: 27.5 mm
Weight: 104 grains
Edge: Reeded
Business strike mintage: 6,146
Proof mintage: None

Like dimes, quarter dollars were not minted until 1796, at which time the Draped Bust obverse style was employed. The obverse features Miss Liberty facing right, with flowing hair and a ribbon behind her head, with drapery covering a plunging neckline. LIBERTY is above and the date 1796 is below. Eight stars are to the left and seven to the right. Around the border are prominent denticles. The reverse has an open wreath tied with a bow at the bottom, enclosing a small eagle perched on a cloud. UNITED STATES OF AMERICA surrounds. There is no indication of value or denomination.

Examples of 1796 quarters are found in all grades, with those from About Good to Fine being most often seen. Probably several hundred survive. Very Fine coins are scarce, Extremely Fine pieces are scarcer yet, and AU or better examples are seldom met with. A number of 1796 quarters were made with prooflike surfaces, such pieces occasionally being called Proof in sale catalogues, although it is not known whether they were specifically made as such. Several dozen prooflike coins exist today. The sharpness of strike on most 1796 quarters encountered is apt to be decent, much more so than on the following design type. An exception is the head of the eagle on the reverse, which is nearly always indistinct.

The 1796 quarter dollar is considered to be a key issue in any grade and is a landmark in the American coinage series.

HALF DOLLAR
1794-1795 Flowing Hair

Designed by: Robert Scot
Issue dates: 1794-1795
Composition: 0.8924 part silver, 0.1076 part copper
Diameter: 32.5 mm
Weight: 208 grains
Edge: Lettered FIFTY CENTS OR HALF A DOLLAR
Business strike mintage: 323,144
Proof mintage: None

Half dollars of the 1794-1795 years bear the same design as contemporary half dimes and silver dollars. The obverse features a small head of Miss Liberty facing right, with flowing hair behind, LIBERTY above, and the date below. Eight stars are to the left and seven to the right. The reverse illustrates an open wreath enclosing a "small" eagle perched on a cloud, with UNITED STATES OF AMERICA surrounding. The borders of this and other half dollars (until over a century later in 1916) have denticles.

Most often encountered among half dollars of this type are pieces dated 1795, these being about 10 times more plentiful than those dated 1794. Examples of both years are apt to be seen in lower grades, from About Good to Fine. Very Fine coins are scarce, Extremely Fine pieces are scarcer yet, and AU coins are rare. Uncirculated examples are seldom met with. Areas of light striking characterize most pieces, as do parallel mint-caused adjustment marks made during the planchet preparation process. As is true of other early issues, these were "workhorse" coins intended for use in the channels of commerce. Few if any pieces were set aside for collectors at the time of issue. Numerous die varieties exist among early half dollars and are described in a book on the subject by Al C. Overton (refer to the bibliography).

HALF DOLLAR
1796-1797 Draped Bust, Small Eagle

Designed by: Robert Scot
Issue dates: 1796-1797
Composition: 0.8924 part silver, 0.1076 copper
Diameter: 32.5 mm
Weight: 208 grains
Edge: Lettered FIFTY CENTS OR HALF A DOLLAR
Business strike mintage: 3,918
Proof mintage: None

This design is similar to that of the other silver denominations of the 1796-1797 years. The obverse depicts Miss Liberty facing right, with flowing hair and a ribbon behind her head, her plunging neckline covered with drapery. LIBERTY is above, and the date is below. Varieties of 1796 exist with 15 and 16 obverse stars, while those of 1797 have 15 stars. The reverse illustrates an open wreath enclosing a small eagle perched on a cloud. UNITED STATES OF AMERICA and the fraction ½ surround.

Of all silver design types, the half dollar style of 1796-1797 is the rarest and most desired, eclipsing even the elusive 1796 quarter. Examples in any grade are few and far between, and even an About Good or a Good half dollar, when described in an auction catalogue, usually furnishes the occasion for a degree of excitement. Most known pieces are in lower grades, About Good to Very Good. Fine pieces are met with less frequency, Very Fine to Extremely Fine coins are rarer still, and coins in AU or better preservation are extreme rarities. Some 1796 half dollars exist with prooflike surfaces. In higher condition levels, while both dates are rare, 1797 is even more so than 1796. A numismatist is apt to find that this particular coin will be the stumbling block or the greatest challenge to finishing an exhibit of United States silver coin design types. Probably about 200 to 300 pieces exist in all grades.

SILVER DOLLAR
1794-1795 Flowing Hair

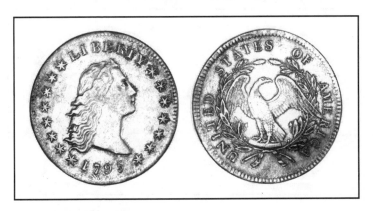

Designed by: Robert Scot
Issue dates: 1794-1795
Composition: 0.8924 part silver, 0.1076 part copper
Diameter: 39 to 40 mm
Weight: 416 grains
Edge: Lettered HUNDRED CENTS ONE DOLLAR OR UNIT
Business strike mintage: 162,053
Proof mintage: None

The Flowing Hair dollar design of 1794-1795 is similar to that used on contemporary half dimes and half dollars. The obverse depicts the small head of Miss Liberty facing right, with flowing hair. LIBERTY is above, and the date is below. Eight stars are to the left and seven are to the right. The reverse depicts an open wreath enclosing a "small" eagle perched on a cloud. UNITED STATES OF AMERICA surrounds. The border of this and other early dollars is composed of denticles.

Mintage records indicate that 1,758 pieces were produced in 1794 and 160,295 in 1795, although it has been suggested that as many as 5,000 to 6,000 of the reported figure for 1795 could have been dated 1794. In any event, 1794 is a major rarity in all grades. The type set collector will probably desire an example dated 1795. Most pieces seen are in grades from About Good to Very Fine. Examples are apt to show mint-caused adjustment marks and to be lightly struck in certain areas. Many hundreds exist, so locating one will be a matter of preference and pocketbook. Extremely Fine pieces are scarce, but still they appear on the market with some frequency. AU coins are rare, and pieces which can be described as strictly Uncirculated are very rare.

SILVER DOLLAR
1795-1798 Draped Bust, Small Eagle

Designed by: Robert Scot
Issue dates; 1795-1798
Composition: 0.8924 part silver, 0.1076 part copper
Diameter: 39 to 40 mm
Weight: 416 grains
Edge: Lettered HUNDRED CENTS ONE DOLLAR OR UNIT
Business strike mintage: 123,434*
Proof mintage: None

The 1795 Draped Bust dollar represents the initial appearance of this design in American coinage. In the silver dollar series the obverse motif was continued through pieces dated 1804 (business strikes last made in 1803, however), while the reverse motif was employed through early 1798. The obverse features a portrait of Miss Liberty as just described, with LIBERTY above, the date below, and eight stars to the left and seven to the right. The reverse shows a "small" eagle perched on a cloud within an open wreath. UNITED STATES OF AMERICA surrounds.

Among early silver dollars, the Draped Bust obverse combined with the Small Eagle reverse may be the scarcest type. Specimens exist in all grades, with those most frequently encountered apt to be in Very Good to Fine preservation. Very Fine pieces can be readily located, Extremely Fine coins are scarcer, and those in AU or better preservation are decidedly rare. A strictly Uncirculated coin would be considered a prime rarity. Examples often show parallel mint-caused adjustment marks. As these coins were produced strictly for utilitarian purposes, no attention was paid to striking them carefully.

*Mintage figure of 123,434 does not include a small number of 1798 dollars with the Small Eagle reverse.

SILVER DOLLAR
1798-1804 Draped Bust, Heraldic Eagle

Designed by: Robert Scot
Issue dates: 1798-1804
Composition: 0.8924 part silver, 0.1076 part copper
Diameter: 39 to 40 mm
Weight: 416 grains
Edge: Lettered HUNDRED CENTS ONE DOLLAR OR UNIT
Business strike mintage: 1,153,709*
Proof mintage: None originally; some restrikes

This style continues the Draped Bust obverse as preceding, except
that the stars have been standardized to seven left and six right, the
only exception being a scarce variety of 1799 with eight left and five
right. The reverse is similar to that used on the dime of the year and
is adapted from the Great Seal of the United States.

Examples of this motif were minted from 1798 through 1803. In
later years, "restrike" pieces were produced dated 1804 as were Proof
restrikes from new dies bearing the dates 1801, 1802, and 1803.
Among business strikes, examples most often encountered are apt
to be dated 1798 or 1799. Those dated 1800 are scarcer, while those
dated from 1801 through 1803 are considerably scarcer, although they
are not rarities. Grades found usually range from Very Good through
Very Fine. Extremely Fine coins are fairly scarce, while AU pieces
are scarcer yet. Strictly Uncirculated coins are great rarities. In keeping with other early silver issues, pieces often display mint-caused
planchet or adjustment marks and areas of light striking.

*Mintage figure of 1,153,709 includes a limited number of 1798 dollars with the earlier Small Eagle reverse.

Chapter 3

New Issues
COPPER AND SILVER 1800-1830

The most difficult era behind us, we now enter the 1800 to 1830 decades of American copper and silver coinage. The Draped Bust obverse motif, which first appeared on the silver dollar in 1795, appeared for the first time in the half cent series on issues dated 1800. The same obverse made its appearance in combination with Heraldic Eagle reverse in the half dime denomination the same year and on quarters and half dollars in 1804 and 1801 respectively. In the field of copper coinage, the Classic Head is found on half cents beginning in 1809 and large cents in 1808, to be followed in the latter series by the so-called Matron Head produced from 1816 onward. The Capped Bust motif appeared on half dimes beginning in 1829, dimes starting in 1809, quarters from 1815 onward, and on half dollars beginning in 1807.

Happily for the numismatist, there are no great stumbling blocks to completing a type set of this era, although the 1800-1805 half dime with Draped Bust obverse and Heraldic Eagle reverse is fairly scarce, and if any type were to be designated a "key" issue in this span, it would be this one.

Coinage of all types was accomplished at the Philadelphia Mint. By 1800, the uncertainty of metal supplies, primarily copper, was not completely solved, but the situation was much less intense than it was earlier. The result was that planchets used on coinage of the new design were apt to be smoother and with fewer defects than earlier. Adjustment marks are still to be seen on certain silver issues of this era. This practice was caused by producing planchets or coinage blanks slightly heavier than the standard weight, and then employing a gallery full of women to weigh each piece individually and file away any unneeded metal. This was more feasible than trying to manufacture planchets of precise weight by cutting them from strips, for such planchets, when slightly underweight, would have to be discarded, as there was no practical way of adding metal to

The Classic Head design, as shown above on an 1810/09 overdate large cent, was employed on cents from 1808 through 1814 and on half cents from 1809 through 1836.

The Capped Bust design, by John Reich, as used on an 1810 half dollar, the general style minted from 1807 through 1836. Produced in large quantities, such coins were used in bank-to-bank transactions, with the result that high grade examples are readily obtained today.

them. So, by making the planchets slightly heavier than needed, they could be adjusted to precision.

Toward the end of the 1800-1830 era, coin collecting achieved some measure of popularity, with such numismatists as Joseph J. Mickley and Robert Gilmor forming cabinets. Occasionally numismatists received selected specimens from the Mint; pieces which had been set aside at the time of coinage or which had been specially produced. Relatively few Proofs were made, and the survival of Uncirculated or Proof pieces was more a matter of chance than intent.

As the Mint produced coins in response to demand for them in the channels of commerce, there were many years in which certain denominations were not struck. For example, among Classic Head half cents mintage was accomplished from 1809 through 1811, after which there was an intermission until 1825, with another hiatus from 1830 onward (although a few pieces were produced in 1831 and 1836). Half dimes of the Heraldic Eagle style were minted from 1800 to 1805, after which no pieces of this denomination were struck until the Capped Bust motif made its appearance in 1829. Quarter dollars were not made from 1797 until 1804, during which latter year the Draped Bust obverse was combined with the Heraldic Eagle reverse. Quarter dollars of this new style were made from 1804 through 1807, followed by a lapse in coinage until the Capped Bust motif appeared in 1815. No new designs of silver dollars were produced during the 1800-1830 years. The most prolific coinage of the period was reserved for cents, which filled an important purpose in everyday commercial transactions, and for half dollars, particularly of the Capped Bust style (1807-1836), which were stored in quantities and used in bank-to-bank transactions. As many if not most half dollars minted during this span were used in bulk transactions, many survive in higher grades, with the result that numerous pieces seen today are in Extremely Fine or better preservation.

HALF CENT
1800-1808 Draped Bust

Designed by: Robert Scot
Issue dates: 1800-1808
Composition: Copper
Diameter: 23.5 mm
Weight: 84 grains
Edge: Plain
Business strike mintage: 3,416,950
Proof mintage: None

The Draped Bust obverse, earlier used on silver dollars beginning in 1795 and on certain other early denominations beginning in 1796, did not appear on the half cent until 1800. Undoubtedly it would have appeared earlier had coinage of half cents not been suspended during the 1798-1799 years. The obverse depicts Miss Liberty facing right, with flowing hair and a ribbon behind her head, her plunging neckline covered with drapery. LIBERTY is above, and the date is below. The reverse comprises an open wreath enclosing HALF CENT, with UNITED STATES OF AMERICA and 1/200 around the border. The edges of these and all later half cents are plain.

Produced in relatively large quantities for the time, half cents of the 1800-1808 years are easy to find today, particularly in the normally encountered grades of Good through Very Fine. Extremely Fine coins are scarce, though not rare, and even AU pieces can be acquired without difficulty. Uncirculated coins are quite elusive and usually are of the dates 1804 or 1806, particularly the latter, for small hoards of these dates turned up many years ago. In keeping with other coinage of the era, striking was apt to be casual at best, with the result that specimens may have some areas of weakness. The planchet quality was considerably improved from the half cents of an earlier era, with the result that without difficulty you can acquire a coin with smooth surfaces. The coloration of a typical half cent of the era is often light, medium, or dark brown. There are many individual differences.

HALF CENT
1809-1836 Classic Head

Designed by: John Reich
Issue dates: 1809-1836
Composition: Copper
Diameter: 23.5 mm
Weight: 84 grains
Edge: Plain
Business strike mintage: 3,635,712
Approximate Proof mintage: 100 to 200, mostly restrikes

The so-called Classic Head design by John Reich made its appearance on half cents in 1809, postdating by one year its debut in the large cent series. A somewhat related motif was used years later on the $2½ and $5 gold coins of 1834. Miss Liberty faces left. Her hair is in curls, close to her head, and is secured by a band inscribed LIBERTY. Seven stars are to the left and six to the right. The date is below. The reverse consists of a continuous wreath tied at the bottom with a ribbon, enclosing HALF CENT at the center, with UNITED STATES OF AMERICA around the border.

Specimens of this type are readily available in all grades from Good through Uncirculated, although, interestingly enough, specimens in Good to Very Good grade are scarcer than those in Fine through Extremely Fine, for at the time of issue half cents did not circulate extensively, so they were not subject to as much wear as were contemporary large cents, for example. Uncirculated coins can be obtained of a number of dates within this span, but the most often seen are those of 1828, 1833, and 1835. Such pieces, if they have original mint red, are apt to have flecks or spots as a result of dampness. Beware of cleaned or "processed" pieces masking as "Uncirculated," for such pieces abound.

1831 and 1836 are exceedingly rare; most known specimens are Proofs, many of them being restrikes. Original Proofs were struck of certain dates toward the end of the era, and all are very difficult to locate.

CENT
1808-1814 Classic Head

Designed by: John Reich
Issue dates: 1808-1814
Composition: Copper
Diameter: 29 mm
Weight: 168 grains
Edge: Plain
Business strike mintage: 4,757,722
Proof mintage: None

The design of the Classic Head large cent is similar to that of the related half cent. The obverse features Miss Liberty, her hair close to her head, with a headband inscribed LIBERTY. Seven stars are to the left and six to the right. The date is below. The reverse displays a continuous wreath tied with a ribbon below, enclosing ONE CENT, with UNITED STATES OF AMERICA surrounding.

There are no major rarities among the 1808-1814 dates, although cents of 1809 are considered to be scarcer than the others. Specimens are readily encountered in all grades from About Good to Extremely Fine. AU examples are rare, and Uncirculated pieces are few and far between. Most examples encountered of the earlier years, 1808 through 1812, are apt to show lightness of strike in certain areas, and even 1813 is not immune from this. In general, 1814 cents are better struck. The planchet coloration also varies, with the earlier years in the 1808-1814 span often being a light to medium brown, with later years being dark brown or black. Often the surfaces are microscopically granular. With some searching, you will have no difficulty in locating an attractive Very Fine to Extremely Fine specimen to illustrate the type, although finding a sharply struck piece on a smooth planchet may be a different proposition entirely.

CENT
1816-1837 Matron Head

Designed by: Robert Scot
Issue dates: 1816-1837, plus 1839/6 overdate
Composition: Copper
Diameter: 28 to 29 mm
Weight: 168 grains
Edge: Plain
Business strike mintage: 47,765,912*
Proof mintage: A few hundred

The so-called Matron Head copper was produced in several variations from 1816 through 1837 (plus 1839/6). Miss Liberty is restyled and now sports a serious, even severe mien. Her hair is tied behind her head in a bun, with two *plain* cords, with additional tresses hanging downward. In her hair a diadem or coronet is inscribed LIBERTY. Thirteen stars surround, interrupted by the date at the bottom. The reverse is stylistically similar to that used in 1808-1814 and consists of a continuous wreath tied with a ribbon, enclosing ONE CENT, with UNITED STATES OF AMERICA surrounding. This particular obverse style was used only on large cents and, unlike certain other large cent motifs, had no counterpart in the half cent series. In 1835 the head was slightly restyled; the change is most obvious at the point of the neck truncation. This new style is found on some 1835, all 1836 (and 1839/6) and some 1837 pieces and is distinguished by the small tip to the neck.

Specimens may be readily located in all grades from About Good to Uncirculated, although Uncirculated pieces are apt to be dated 1816 through 1820, particularly the years 1818 and 1820, remnants from the so-called Randall Hoard dispersed in the late 19th century. The quality of striking, smoothness of the surface, and other characteristics vary from date to date and variety to variety.

*Mintage figure of 47,765,912 does not include 1837 cents of this style.

HALF DIME
1800-1805 Draped Bust, Heraldic Eagle

Designed by: Robert Scot
Issue dates: 1800-1805
Composition: 0.8924 part silver, 0.1076 part copper
Diameter: 16.5 mm
Weight: 20.8 grains
Edge: Reeded
Business strike mintage: 124,270
Proof mintage: None

The half dimes of the 1800-1805 years continued the Draped Bust obverse used earlier in 1796-1797, except that the stars beginning in 1800 have been standardized to seven left and six right. The reverse is of the Heraldic Eagle style adopted from the Great Seal of the United States and used beginning in the preceding decade on certain other silver denominations. At the center is an eagle with a shield on its breast, holding in its beak a ribbon inscribed E PLURIBUS UNUM and grasping in its talon a bundle of arrows and an olive branch. Above the eagle is an arc of clouds under which is a group of stars. UNITED STATES OF AMERICA surrounds. No mark of denomination or value appears on the coin.

Half dimes of this era are scarce, with 1802 being a prime rarity. Most surviving examples of various 1800-1805 dates are seen in lower ranges of condition, from About Good to Very Good or so. Fine specimens are not easy to locate, Very Fine pieces are still more elusive, and Extremely Fine coins are rare. Strictly Uncirculated pieces are extremely rare. Those that do come on the market are apt to be dated 1800. Uncirculated specimens dated 1801, 1802, and 1803 (no pieces were coined in 1804), and 1805 are exceedingly rare or nonexistent. Nearly all known specimens exhibit a degree of light striking in one area or another, particularly on the high points of Miss Liberty's hair, among the obverse stars, and on the reverse among the stars above the eagle. Such striking characteristics are to be expected, and a numismatist seeking a perfectly struck, extremely sharp example in a high grade is apt to never encounter such a coin!

HALF DIME
Capped Bust 1829-1837

Designed by: William Kneass adapting the design of John Reich
Issue dates: 1829-1837
Composition: 0.8924 part silver, 0.1076 part copper
Diameter: 15.5 mm
Weight: 20.8 grains
Edge: Reeded
Business strike mintage: 13,058,700
Proof mintage: Several hundred

Following a span of years from 1806 to 1828, when no half dimes were minted, the Capped Bust style was introduced in 1829. The design is quite similar to that used on the half dollar 1807-1836, by John Reich, and was modified from that source by William Kneass, Mint engraver. The obverse features Miss Liberty facing to the left, her hair covered by a cloth cap secured by a band inscribed LIBERTY, with tresses flowing down to her shoulder. Her neckline is draped with a gown, secured with a brooch at the shoulder. Seven stars are to the left and six to the right. The date is below. The reverse features an eagle with the shield on its breast, perched on a branch and holding arrows, with E PLURIBUS UNUM on a scroll above, and UNITED STATES OF AMERICA and 5 C. surrounding.

The span of coinage from 1829 through 1837 contains no rare dates (although some individual die varieties within the dates are elusive), so the type set collector has his choice of the entire range. Specimens seen today are most often encountered in grades from Very Good through Very Fine, and these are fairly plentiful. Extremely Fine and AU pieces can also be found with frequency. Uncirculated coins are scarcer yet, with truly Gem Uncirculated pieces being elusive. Most issues within the range are well struck, so it is possible to pick the grade you want and acquire a piece with excellent design detail definition.

DIME
1809-1827 Capped Bust, Open Collar

Designed by: John Reich
Issue dates: 1809-1827
Composition: 0.8924 part silver, 0.1076 part copper
Diameter: 18.8 mm (with some variation)
Weight: 41.6 grains
Edge: Reeded
Business Strike mintage: 4,931,844
Proof mintage: Fewer than 150

In 1809 the Capped Bust dime made its appearance. The design is similar to that used on earlier half dollars beginning in 1807. The obverse features Miss Liberty with her hair in a cloth cap secured by a band inscribed LIBERTY, with tresses flowing down to her shoulder. Her bust is draped in a cloth or gown secured by a clasp or brooch. Seven stars are to the left and six to the right. The date is below. The reverse depicts an eagle perched on a branch and holding arrows, E PLURIBUS UNUM is on a scroll above, and UNITED STATES OF AMERICA and 10 C. appear around the border. The planchet diameter is approximately 18.8 mm, which distinguishes it from the small planchet (approximately 17.9 mm) format, struck in a closed collar, introduced in 1828.

Coinage during the 1809-1827 years was intermittent; some years were skipped. Specimens of commoner dates are readily encountered in various grades from Good to Very Fine. Extremely Fine pieces can be found without difficulty, as can AU coins. Uncirculated pieces, particularly finer examples of these, are quite rare. Striking is apt to vary from issue to issue, and finding one with excellent definition of detail will not be easy.

DIME
1828-1837 Capped Bust, Closed Collar

Designed by: John Reich (adapted from)
Issue dates: 1828-1837
Composition: 0.9824 part silver, 0.1076 part copper
Diameter: 17.9 mm (with some variation)
Weight: 41.6 grains
Edge: Reeded
Business strike mintage: 6,778,350
Proof mintage: Fewer than 200

This variety is an adaptation of the previous 1809-1827 style and is the same except for certain minor modifications. The diameter is slightly smaller, and the border has denticles spaced closer together than on the previous type (although some transitional pieces have the old denticle style). The stars are slightly smaller, and there is some subtle restyling. Dimes of this format were made from 1828 through 1837 inclusive. No dates are rarities, although there are several elusive varieties within the range. Examples are available in all grades from Good through Uncirculated, with Very Good to Very Fine being the most often seen. Uncirculated pieces are elusive, and ones in higher states of the Uncirculated category are rare.

QUARTER DOLLAR
1804-1807 Draped Bust, Heraldic Eagle

Designed by: Robert Scot
Issue dates: 1804-1807
Composition: 0.8924 part silver, 0.1076 part copper
Diameter: 27.5 mm
Weight: 104 grains
Edge: Reeded
Business strike mintage: 554,900
Proof mintage: None

Quarter dollars minted from 1804 through 1807 continue the Draped Bust obverse first used in 1796. Miss Liberty faces to the right, her hair is in tresses behind her head, with a ribbon at the back of her head, and with a drapery or gown covering her low neckline. Seven stars are to the left and six to the right. LIBERTY is above and the date is below. The reverse is an adaptation of the Great Seal of the United States and features an eagle with a shield on its breast, E PLURIBUS UNUM on a scroll or ribbon in its beak, and its talons grasping a bundle of arrows and a branch. Above the eagle is an arc of clouds with stars below. UNITED STATES OF AMERICA and 25 C. surrounds.

Examples of the 1804-1807 years are readily located in grades from About Good through Very Fine. Extremely Fine pieces are elusive, AU pieces are rare, and Uncirculated pieces are exceedingly rare. Virtually without exception, issues of this design are lightly struck in one or more areas, with the obverse and reverse rims, the stars on the obverse, and the stars above the eagle on the reverse being typical areas of light impression. The same situation is shared with the half dimes, dimes, half dollars of this date range.

QUARTER DOLLAR
1815-1828 Capped Bust, Large Diameter

Designed by: John Reich
Issue dates: 1815-1828
Composition: 0.8924 part silver, 0.1076 part copper
Diameter: 27 mm
Weight: 104 grains
Edge: Reeded
Business strike mintage: 1,290,584
Proof mintage: Fewer than 100

Following a suspension of quarter dollar coinage after 1807, the denomination was again produced in 1815, which time the Capped Bust style was introduced. The motifs are similar to that found on other silver denominations of the era. The obverse depicts Miss Liberty facing left, wearing a cloth cap secured with a band inscribed LIBERTY, with tresses flowing to her shoulder. Her plunging neckline is draped in cloth and is secured by a brooch or a clasp at the shoulder. Seven stars are to the left and six are to the right. The date is below. The reverse shows an eagle perched on a branch and holding three arrows, a shield on its breast, and E PLURIBUS UNUM on a scroll above. UNITED STATES OF AMERICA and 25 C. appear around the border.

While several dates within this range are scarce, and the 1823/2 and 1827 are major rarities, the type set collector will have no difficulty acquiring one of the more plentiful issues. Typically encountered specimens are apt to range from Very Good to Very Fine preservation. While they are not as easily located as half dollars of the same years and designs, still there are enough around that acquiring one will be no problem. Extremely Fine specimens are scarce, AU pieces are scarcer yet, and strictly Uncirculated coins are rare. Striking quality varies from issue to issue, and many show weaknesses in certain areas, although with some searching you should be able to buy a well defined piece.

HALF DOLLAR
1801-1807 Draped Bust, Heraldic Eagle

Designed by: Robert Scot
Issue dates: 1801-1807
Composition: 0.8924 part silver, 0.1076 part copper
Diameter: 32.5 mm
Weight: 208 grains
Edge: Lettered FIFTY CENTS OR HALF A DOLLAR
Business strike mintage: 1,600,787
Proof mintage: None

Half dollars minted from 1801 through 1807 continue the Draped Bust obverse motif introduced in 1796. In 1801 the stars were standardized to a count of 13, with seven to the left and six to the right. Miss Liberty appears facing right, her hair flowing behind her head and, tied with a ribbon bow. Her low neckline is covered by a gown or drapery. LIBERTY is above and the date is below. The reverse is an adaptation of the Great Seal of the United States and consists of an eagle with a shield on its breast, holding arrows and an olive branch, and with a scroll inscribed E PLURIBUS UNUM in its beak. Above the eagle is an arc of clouds below which is a group of stars. UNITED STATES OF AMERICA surrounds.

There are no rare dates within the 1801-1807 span, although some varieties are elusive. Nearly all specimens encountered display weakness of striking in one area or another, with the quality of strike becoming less and less as the years advanced. Nearly all seen with the dates of 1806 and, particularly, 1807 show weakness. Specimens are typically found in grades from Very Good to Very Fine, although Extremely Fine pieces are found with some frequency. AU pieces are scarce, and strictly Uncirculated coins are rare. Even an Uncirculated specimen of 1807, for example, is apt to be very weakly defined in such areas as the rims, the obverse and reverse stars, and parts of the eagle.

HALF DOLLAR
1807-1836 Capped Bust, Lettered Edge

Designed by: John Reich
Issue dates: 1807-1836
Composition: 0.9824 part silver, 0.1076 part copper
Diameter: 32.5 mm
Weight: 208 grains
Edge: Lettered FIFTY CENTS OR HALF A DOLLAR
Business strike mintage: 82,339,124
Proof mintage: 200 to 300

In 1807 the Capped Bust obverse was introduced. Miss Liberty faces left. She wears a cap secured at the base with a ribbon or band inscribed LIBERTY, with tresses falling to her shoulder. Her low neckline is draped in a cloth or a gown and is secured by a brooch on her shoulder. Seven stars are to the left and six are to the right. The date is below. The reverse depicts an eagle perched on an olive branch and holding three arrows, with E PLURIBUS UNUM above on a scroll and UNITED STATES OF AMERICA 50 C. surrounding.

Although there are a number of scarce varieties in the 1807-1836 range, most are readily obtainable. Specimens of most issues are typically encountered in grades from Fine to Extremely Fine, with some of the earlier dates in the range, 1807 through 1820, sometimes seen in Good to Very Good preservation. AU pieces are not difficult to find, especially of dates in the late 1820s and 1830s. Uncirculated coins, particularly ones in higher ranges of that category are elusive, with superb pieces being rare. Many examples show lightness of striking, particularly on the stars on the obverse, the high parts of Miss Liberty, and E PLURIBUS UNUM on the reverse. Among Uncirculated pieces, examples typically have friction or rubbing at the lower left of the bust, from coin-to-coin contact in bank bags.

Chapter 4

New Issues
COPPER AND SILVER 1831-1850

The 20 years from 1831 through 1850 saw many changes in the coinage spectrum. Whereas the Philadelphia Mint satisfied production needs from 1793 onward, by 1838 the opening of the American West called for a branch mint at New Orleans, located at the gateway to the vast Mississippi River trading area. At the same time, additional branches were opened at Dahlonega, Georgia and Charlotte, North Carolina, these last two for production of gold coins from native metal. In 1854 the San Francisco Mint came on stream. The "S" mintmark found its place on numerous coin designs which were earlier initiated during the 1831-1850 span.

In 1836, steam-powered presses were brought to the Philadelphia Mint to replace horse-powered devices of the early years. New advances in metal preparation and planchet cutting and adjustment contributed to increased efficiency of production. After 1836, coinage was more mechanical, with the result that pieces after that date are more uniform in appearance and less subject to striking variations.

The half cent and cent saw the advent of the Braided Hair motif which was continued through 1857. The Capped Bust design is found on several silver issues, but among silver denominations most display a new style, the Liberty Seated motif.

Using sketches made by Thomas Sully, Mint engraver Christian Gobrecht introduced the Liberty Seated design on silver dollars of 1836 (see Chapter 12). In 1837 the first Liberty Seated coins were made for circulation, dimes and half dimes. The first issues had starless obverse fields, a short-lived situation, as stars were added the following year. Although no one could have anticipated it at the time, as the 19th century continued onward the Liberty Seated motif became widespread across nearly all silver denominations. When the style was finally discontinued in 1891, it marked the passing of a memorable era. In the meantime, the Liberty Seated design

This 1846 large cent illustrates the Braided Hair motif utilized on cents from 1839 through 1857 and half cents from 1840 through 1857. A somewhat related, but differently styled design is found on contemporary gold coins of the $2½, $5, and $10 denominations.

The Liberty Seated design, shown above on an 1846 silver dollar, was used on silver denominations from the half dime through the dollar. The work of Mint engraver Christian Gobrecht, the motif was conceived in 1835-1836 and made its first regular appearance in the silver dollar denomination in 1840, following production of patterns dated 1836, 1838, and 1839.

was found on many other products, including advertisements for fireworks, fabrics, and commercial emblems.

The new issues of the 1831-1850 era contain no great rarities so far as type set collectors are concerned, although a few are moderately scarce, particularly in higher grades.

The appreciation of any type set can be enhanced by relating it to contemporary history. For example, the 1831 through 1850 years saw discoveries in the West, the Panic of 1837 and the consequent Hard Times era, the beginnings of the Gold Rush in California, endless bickering about the slavery question, and enough political activity to keep 18 research scholars at Harvard busy 10 years delving into it all!

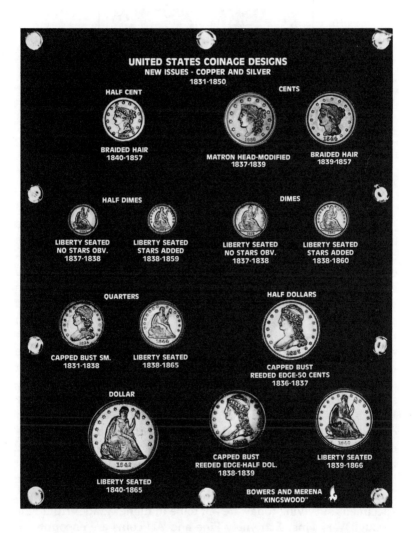

UNITED STATES COINAGE DESIGNS
NEW ISSUES - COPPER AND SILVER
1831-1850

HALF CENT

CENTS

BRAIDED HAIR
1840-1857

MATRON HEAD-MODIFIED
1837-1839

BRAIDED HAIR
1839-1857

HALF DIMES

DIMES

LIBERTY SEATED
NO STARS OBV.
1837-1838

LIBERTY SEATED
STARS ADDED
1838-1859

LIBERTY SEATED
NO STARS OBV.
1837-1838

LIBERTY SEATED
STARS ADDED
1838-1860

QUARTERS

HALF DOLLARS

CAPPED BUST SM.
1831-1838

LIBERTY SEATED
1838-1865

CAPPED BUST
REEDED EDGE-50 CENTS
1836-1837

DOLLAR

CAPPED BUST
REEDED EDGE-HALF DOL.
1838-1839

LIBERTY SEATED
1839-1866

LIBERTY SEATED
1840-1865

BOWERS AND MERENA
"KINGSWOOD"

New copper and silver designs introduced during the 1831-1850 years are housed in the ''Kingswood'' display holder shown above. Telling as they do the history of coinage over the years, displays featuring coins by design types have won many prizes at numismatic conventions and exhibitions.

HALF CENT
1840-1857 Braided Hair

Designed by: Christian Gobrecht
Issue dates: 1840-1857
Composition: Copper
Diameter: 23 mm
Weight: 84 grains
Edge: Plain
Business strike mintage: 544,510
Proof mintage: Fewer than 1,500, combined originals and restrikes

In 1840 a new half cent design, the Braided Hair style, made its appearance. However, there was not a demand for new pieces in the channels of commerce, for the Treasury had vast stores of undistributed earlier coins upon which it could draw, so no new half cents were struck for circulation until 1849. Specimens of the 1840-1848 years were limited to Proofs made for collectors. The obverse design depicts a trim head of Miss Liberty facing left, her hair in a bun tied with two beaded cords, and with the word LIBERTY on a diadem or coronet. Tresses hang downward to her neck. Surrounding the obverse border are 13 stars and the date. The reverse design is somewhat similar to the style used on half cents of the 1809-1836 era and consists of a continuous wreath tied with a ribbon below, enclosing HALF CENT, with UNITED STATES OF AMERICA around the border, although the details are slightly different from those used earlier. Half cents were produced in quantities for circulation from 1849 through 1851 and again from 1853 through 1857. In the latter year the denomination was discontinued. As half cents did not circulate extensively, particularly during the era of the Braided Hair design, specimens surviving today are apt to be in higher grades from Fine through Very Fine. Extremely Fine and AU coins are encountered with some frequency. Uncirculated pieces are scarce, and truly superb Uncirculated coins are very scarce.

CENT
1837-1839 Matron Head Modified

Designed by: Christian Gobrecht
Issue dates: 1837-1839
Composition: Copper
Diameter: 27.5 mm
Weight: 168 grains
Edge: Plain
Business strike mintage: 15,057,161*
Proof mintage: Fewer than 100

Cents of the 1837-1839 years, conveniently grouped under the "Matron Head Modified" heading, actually consist of a number of obverse styles. All have in common the head of Miss Liberty facing left, her hair tied in a bun, with tresses hanging to her neck, and with the word LIBERTY on a diadem or coronet. Thirteen stars surround, and the date is below. Typically the reverse displays a continuous wreath with ribbon at the bottom, enclosing ONE CENT and with UNITED STATES OF AMERICA surrounding. Variations of the era are usually catalogued by the obverse and include such styles as 1837 and 1838 with "Head of 1838," with *beaded* cords holding the hair bun; the 1839 "Silly Head," and the 1839 "Booby Head." The 1839/6 overdate, with *plain* hair cords, is part of the earlier listed 1816-1837 style.

Examples are available in all grades of various issues, the commonest being 1838, with Very Good to Very Fine being the most often seen. Extremely Fine coins are readily available, as are AU pieces. Uncirculated coins are more often seen for 1837 and 1838 than for 1839. For all years, superb Uncirculated pieces are rare. The sharpness of striking varies from issue to issue, but with some patience it is possible to acquire specimens with reasonably good definition of the stars and wreath.

*Mintage figure of 15,057,161 includes the 1839 Braided Hair cent.

CENT
1839-1857 Braided Hair

Designed by: Christian Gobrecht
Issue dates: 1839-1857
Composition: Copper
Diameter: 27.5 mm
Weight: 168 grains
Edge: Plain
Business strike mintage: 70,916,803*
Proof mintage: Fewer than 1,000

The Braided Hair cent is similar in design to the half cent of the same style and features a compact head of Miss Liberty, her hair-strands sharply defined and tied in the back in a bun secured by two beaded cords. A diadem or coronet bears the inscription LIBERTY. Thirteen stars surround, and the date is below. The reverse shows a continous wreath tied with a ribbon at the bottom, ONE CENT within, with UNITED STATES OF AMERICA around the border. The details on the reverse are slightly different from that used earlier, but the style is the same. Although there are no rare dates from 1839 through 1857, several varieties are scarce, as is the last date of issue, 1857. By that time the large cent was viewed as being cumbersome for use in everyday transactions, and the Mint desired to replace it with a smaller and more easily handled coin (the result being the Flying Eagle cent subsequently introduced). Typical specimens encountered are apt to range in grade from Very Good to Very Fine, although Extremely Fine coins are plentiful and AU pieces are readily available. Uncirculated coins are also available, although ones in the higher ranges of the category and with full mint color are decidedly elusive.

*Mintage figure of 70,916,803 does not include the 1839 cents.

HALF DIME
1837-1838 Liberty Seated, No Stars

Designed by: Christian Gobrecht
Issue dates: 1837 (Philadelphia) and 1838-O (New Orleans)
Composition: .900 part silver, .100 part copper
Diameter: 15.5 mm
Weight: 20.625 grains
Edge: Reeded
Business strike mintage: 1,475,000
Proof mintage: Fewer than 50

Christian Gobrecht's Liberty Seated motif, used on half dimes from 1837 through the end of the series in 1873, was produced in 1837 at the Philadelphia Mint and 1838 at the New Orleans Mint, in the format *without obverse stars*, thus isolating these two issues as a separate type. The obverse depicts Miss Liberty seated on a rock, her left hand holding a liberty cap on a pole and her right hand holding a shield inscribed LIBERTY. The date is at the bottom border. The reverse consists of an open wreath tied with a ribbon, enclosing HALF DIME, with UNITED STATES OF AMERICA surrounding. Mintage figures reveal that 1,405,000 of the 1837 Philadelphia issue were produced while only 70,000 were made of the 1838-O.

Specimens are readily obtainable in grades from Good through Extremely Fine. The type collector will direct his attention to the 1837, for in every grade the 1838-O is considerably more expensive. In AU and Uncirculated preservation the Philadelphia coin is available without difficulty, although higher grade Uncirculated pieces are quite elusive. Uncirculated examples of 1838-O are exceedingly rare. The design without stars was used on circulating coinage only in the half dime and dime series and not on the quarter or half dollar (in the dollar series the without-stars motif appears only in pattern form in 1836).

HALF DIME
1838-1859 Liberty Seated, With Stars

Designed by: Christian Gobrecht
Issue dates: 1838-1859
Composition: .900 silver, .100 copper
Diameter: 15.5
Weight: 20.625 grains 1838 to 1853 No Arrows; 19.2 grains later
Edge: Reeded
Business strike mintage: 42,705,774
Proof mintage: Fewer than 1,500 pieces

In 1838 stars were added to the obverse of the Liberty Seated design. Otherwise, the motif is similar to the 1837 and 1838-O Liberty
Seated pieces. From 1838 through 1859 many different varieties were
produced, including some struck at the New Orleans Mint (and bearing a distinctive O mintmark on the reverse). Early issues lack drapery at Miss Liberty's elbow. There are some scarce dates and varieties within the range, notably 1846, 1849-O, and 1853-O without
arrows at date, but there are enough common varieties that it is not
difficult to acquire an example in Good to Very Fine preservation at
reasonable cost. Extremely Fine coins abound, and AU examples can
be obtained easily. Uncirculated pieces are scarce, and higher echelon Uncirculated coins are scarcer yet. Although the general Liberty
Seated type with obverse stars was minted from 1838 through 1859,
certain specimens of 1853 and all of those dated 1854 and 1855 were
produced with arrowheads at the date and represent a distinctive
type discussed in the following chapter.

DIME
1837-1838 Liberty Seated, No Stars

Designed by: Christian Gobrecht
Issue dates: 1837 (Philadelphia) 1838-O (New Orleans)
Composition: 0.900 part silver, 0.100 part copper
Diameter: 17.9 mm
Weight: 41.25 grains
Edge: Reeded
Business strike mintage: 1,088,534
Proof mintage: Fewer than 50 pieces

The first Liberty Seated dime variety is without obverse stars and closely parallels the half dime of the same era. Indeed, the mintage was accomplished similarly: pieces were struck only at the Philadelphia Mint in 1837 and only at the New Orleans Mint in 1838. Some 682,500 were struck at the former facility and 408,034 at the latter. The device consists of Miss Liberty seated on a rock, holding in her left hand a liberty cap on a pole, and holding a shield with her right. The date is below. The reverse displays an open wreath enclosing ONE DIME, with UNITED STATES OF AMERICA surrounding. As attractive as this cameo-like motif is to collectors today, Mint officials did not consider it to be desirable, and it was discontinued shortly thereafter.

The type set enthusiast will find that examples of either issue are readily available in grades from Good through Very Fine or so, with the 1838-O being a bit more expensive. Extremely Fine and AU coins are also encountered with regularity, less so for 1838-O. Uncirculated pieces, when found, are nearly always dated 1837. Those dated 1838-O are great rarities. Superb Uncirculated coins are quite elusive.

DIME
1838-1860 Liberty Seated With Stars

Designed by: Christian Gobrecht
Issue dates: 1838-1860
Composition: 0.900 part silver, 0.100 part copper
Diameter: 17.9 mm
Weight: 41.2 grains 1838 to 1853 no arrows; 38.4 grains later
Edge: Reeded
Business strike mintage: 42,962,915
Proof mintage: Fewer than 1,500 pieces

In 1838, stars were added to the obverse of the Liberty Seated motif. This style was continued through 1859, plus 1860 at the San Francisco Mint only. The reverse is similar to the preceding but the wreath on the later issues is slightly heavier. Early issues lack drapery at Miss Liberty's elbow.

The type set collector has his choice of numerous varieties within this span, including a number of New Orleans and San Francisco Mint pieces. While issues such as 1844, 1845-O, 1846, and certain San Francisco pieces are rare, enough common issues exist that no difficulty will be experienced in acquiring a typical example from Good to Extremely Fine grade. AU pieces are slightly harder to find, and Uncirculated coins are scarcer still. Superb Uncirculated pieces are quite elusive. As is the case with half dimes, certain dimes of 1853 and all dimes of 1854 and 1855 have arrows at the date and are considered to be separate types (discussed in the following chapter).

QUARTER DOLLAR
1831-1838 Capped Bust, Small Diameter

Designed by: Willian Kneass (after John Reich)
Issue dates: 1831-1838
Composition: 0.8924 part silver, 0.1076 part copper
Diameter: 24.3 mm
Weight: 104 grains
Edge: Reeded
Business strike mintage: 4,202,400
Proof mintage: Fewer than 150

Following a lapse of coinage of quarter dollars for two years, the denomination was again produced in 1831. Employed was a revised version of John Reich's Capped Bust style introduced in 1815. The 1831-1838 version is of smaller diameter and has restyled features, letters, stars, and numerals, giving the piece a more cameo-like appearance than its predecessor. The obverse depicts Miss Liberty facing left, wearing a cloth cap secured by a band inscribed LIBERTY, with tresses flowing to her shoulder. Her neckline is draped in a gown secured by a brooch or clasp. Seven stars are to the left and six to the right. The date is below. The reverse shows an eagle perched on an olive branch and holding three arrows, with UNITED STATES OF AMERICA above and 25 C. below.

The type set collector has his choice of any date from 1831 through 1838, as all are priced approximately the same in the market, although certain dates, 1835 in particular, are more plentiful than others. Examples are readily found in grades from Very Good through Extremely Fine. AU coins are scarcer, and pieces designated as Uncirculated are rare. Higher echelon Uncirculated pieces are very elusive.

QUARTER DOLLAR
1838-1865 Liberty Seated

Designed by: Christian Gobrecht
Issue dates: 1838-1865
Composition: 0.900 part silver, 0.100 part copper
Diameter: 24.3 mm
Weight: 103.125 grains 1838 to 1853 no arrows; 96 grains later
Edge: Reeded
Business strike mintage: 46,685,313
Proof Mintage: fewer than 5,500

Gobrecht's Liberty Seated design made its appearance in the quarter dollar denomination in 1838. Matching other new silver designs of the time, the quarter dollar depicts Miss Liberty seated on a rock, her left hand holding a liberty cap on a pole and her right holding a shield inscribed LIBERTY. Thirteen stars are at the border, and the date is below. The reverse is somewhat similar to the preceding except the denomination is expressed differently. An eagle is perched on an olive branch and holds three arrows. UNITED STATES OF AMERICA is above and the denomination QUAR. DOL. is below. There is no motto on the reverse. This style was produced from 1838 to early 1853 and again from 1856 through 1865. Early issues lack drapery at Miss Liberty's elbow. From 1853 through 1855 special varieties with arrows at date were made and are different types (as discussed in the following chapter). The collector has a wide variety of type set possibilities within the range. Although there are a number of scarce and rare dates, there are sufficient common issues that there should be no trouble in obtaining coins graded from Good through Extremely Fine, although it is important to note that Liberty Seated quarters of this era are in general scarcer than half dimes, dimes, or half dollars. AU pieces are scarce, and Uncirculated coins are scarcer yet. Superb Uncirculated coins are rare in all instances. Proofs were distributed to the public beginning in 1858.

HALF DOLLAR
1836-1837 Reeded Edge, 50 CENTS

Designed by: Christian Gobrecht
Issue dates: 1836-1837
Composition: 0.900 part silver, 0.100 part copper
Diameter: 30 mm
Weight: 206.25 grains
Edge: Reeded
Business strike mintage: 3,631,020
Proof mintage: Fewer than 40

In 1836, steam-powered presses were introduced to the Philadelphia Mint, and one of the first innovations was a new half dollar format. John Reich's Capped Bust style was modified by Christian Gobrecht. The result was a coin of smaller diameter, with reeded edge, displaying at center the older design of Miss Liberty facing left, wearing a cloth cap with a band inscribed LIBERTY, with tresses falling to her shoulder, and with her bosom draped in a gown secured by a brooch. Six stars are to the left and seven to the right. The date is below. The reverse depicts an eagle perched on a branch and holding three arrows with UNITED STATES OF AMERICA above and the denomination expressed as 50 CENTS below.

1836 half dollars of the reeded edge format were produced to the extent of just 1,200 pieces and are rare in all grades today. 1837 half dollars were minted in a quantity of 3,629,820 and are relatively plentiful in grades from Good through Extremely Fine. AU coins are scarce, and strictly Uncirculated pieces are scarcer yet. Superb Uncirculated coins are rare.

HALF DOLLAR
1838-1839 Capped Bust, HALF DOL.

Designed by: Christian Gobrecht
Issue dates: 1838-1839
Composition: 0.900 part silver, 0.100 part copper
Diameter: 30 mm
Weight: 206.25 grains
Edge: Reeded
Business strike mintage: 5,117,972
Proof mintage: Fewer than 50

In 1838 the Capped Bust half dollar was restyled slightly, and the denomination on the reverse, earlier styled as 50 CENTS, was revised to HALF DOL. Certain other changes were affected in the thickness of the reverse letters and the details of the eagle. For the first time, half dollars were struck at a branch mint, New Orleans. The 1838-O half dollar is one of America's prime rarities. It is believed that just 20 were struck, nearly all of which had prooflike surfaces. In the following year, 1839, a more generous mintage of 178,976 half dollars occurred at New Orleans.

The type set collector will probably seek an example of the 1838 or 1839 Philadelphia issue, each of which was minted to the extent of more than a million. Examples are readily available in grades from Very Good through Extremely Fine. AU coins are scarce, and Uncirculated pieces are scarcer yet. Superb Uncirculated coins are very rare and are seldom seen or offered for sale.

HALF DOLLAR
1839-1866 Liberty Seated

Designed by: Christian Gobrecht
Issue dates: 1839-1866
Composition: 0.900 part silver, 0.100 part copper
Diameter: 30.6 mm
Weight: 206.25 grains 1839-1853; 192 grains later
Edge: Reeded
Business strike mintage: 76,238,285
Proof mintage: Fewer than 5,500

The Liberty Seated motif, without motto on the reverse, was minted in the half dollar series from 1839 through 1866. Certain pieces dated 1853 and all dated 1854 and 1855 have arrows at the date and are different types, as discussed in the following chapter. The obverse depicts Miss Liberty seated on a rock, holding in her left hand a liberty cap on a pole and with her right hand holding a shield inscribed LIBERTY. Thirteen stars are above, and the date is below. The reverse is similar to the preceding and consists of an eagle perched on an olive branch and holding three arrows, with UNITED STATES OF AMERICA above and HALF DOL. below. Numerous variations exist throughout the series, including the absence of drapery from Miss Liberty's elbow on certain issues, different sizes of reverse lettering, and different date numeral sizes. Certain pieces dated 1839 lack drapery at Miss Liberty's elbow. While there are some scarce issues within this span, there are enough common varieties that the numismatist will have no difficulty acquiring examples in grades from Good through Extremely Fine. AU coins likewise appear with frequency. Uncirculated pieces are scarcer, and superb Uncirculated coins are quite rare. The quality of striking is apt to vary from issue to issue, with those made in New Orleans being often lightly struck, particularly on the obverse stars.

SILVER DOLLAR
1840-1865 Liberty Seated

Designed by: Christian Gobrecht
Issue dates: 1840-1865
Composition: 0.900 part silver, 0.100 part copper
Diameter: 38.1 mm
Weight: 412.5 grains
Edge: Reeded
Business strike mintage: 2,890,563
Proof mintage: Fewer than 5,500

Following the production of an illustrious series of Liberty Seated pattern dollars in 1836, 1838, and 1839, the Liberty Seated style was first produced for large-scale circulating coinage in 1840. From then through 1865 coinage was continuous. The design parallels that of other Liberty Seated issues. The obverse depicts Miss Liberty seated on a rock, holding in her left hand a liberty cap on a pole and with her right hand holding a shield inscribed LIBERTY. Thirteen stars are above, and the date is below. The reverse shows an eagle perched on an olive branch and holding three arrows, with UNITED STATES OF AMERICA above and HALF DOL. below.

Within the 1840-1865 span there are a number of scarce and rare issues, with 1851, 1852, and 1858 designated as major rarities. Commoner issues are readily available in grades from Very Good through Extremely Fine, with most survivors being in Fine to Very Fine grade. As silver dollars were not circulated as extensively as other denominations, few are seen in grades below Very Good. AU coins are available as are Uncirculated pieces, particularly 1859-O and 1860-O in the latter category (survivors from a small group of coins which came to the light during the Treasury release of 1962). Superb Uncirculated pieces are rarities. Proofs were first distributed to collectors in 1858 and are available from that date through 1865, although scattered earlier issues occasionally come on the market.

Note: See Chapter 12, ''Some Interesting Options,'' for information on the Gobrecht dollars 1836-1839.

Chapter 5

New Issues
COPPER, COPPER-NICKEL, AND SILVER 1851-1860

The decade preceding the Civil War saw many changes in the coinage spectrum. In 1857 the unpopular half cent denomination was phased out, and the old and cumbersome "large" cent was discontinued after a relatively small coinage for the year. In the place of the latter appeared a new format cent, made of copper nickel, of small diameter, featuring a flying eagle on the obverse. Following the production of 600 or more patterns in 1856 (made for distribution to congressmen, newspaper editors, and others of influence), coinage in quantity for circulation commenced in 1857. The Flying Eagle cent, despite its appeal to collectors today, proved short-lived at the time of issue, and after 1858 it was discontinued. In its place appeared still another cent design, this one featuring an Indian head on the obverse. For the first year a laurel wreath was employed as the reverse motif, but in 1860 it was replaced by an oak wreath and shield design.

A new denomination appeared: the silver three-cent piece. The ostensible purpose was to permit the use of a single coin to buy three-cent postage stamps. Three different designs were eventually made of the silver three-cent issues. Interestingly, they all appeared in the 1851-1860 decade. Unlike other silver coins of the era, which were composed of 0.900 part silver and 0.100 part copper, the silver three-cent piece contained 0.750 part silver and 0.250 part copper for the initial type produced from 1851 through 1853. Subsequently, the alloy was changed to conform to the standard of other denominations.

Following the discovery of gold in California in 1848 and the subsequent Gold Rush of the 1849-1850 years, the precious yellow metal became "common" in relation to silver. The historic balance between gold and silver was somewhat upset in world markets, with the result that silver increased in value. By early 1853, United States silver coins were worth more in melt-down value than their face value, with the outcome that millions of dollars' worth were reduced

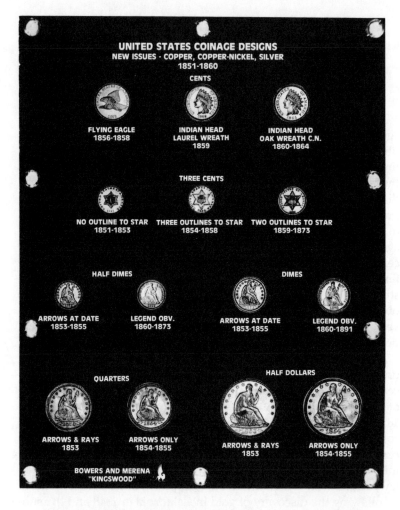

UNITED STATES COINAGE DESIGNS
NEW ISSUES - COPPER, COPPER-NICKEL, SILVER
1851-1860

CENTS

FLYING EAGLE
1856-1858

INDIAN HEAD
LAUREL WREATH
1859

INDIAN HEAD
OAK WREATH C.N.
1860-1864

THREE CENTS

NO OUTLINE TO STAR
1851-1853

THREE OUTLINES TO STAR
1854-1858

TWO OUTLINES TO STAR
1859-1873

HALF DIMES

ARROWS AT DATE
1853-1855

LEGEND OBV.
1860-1873

DIMES

ARROWS AT DATE
1853-1855

LEGEND OBV.
1860-1891

QUARTERS

ARROWS & RAYS
1853

ARROWS ONLY
1854-1855

HALF DOLLARS

ARROWS & RAYS
1853

ARROWS ONLY
1854-1855

BOWERS AND MERENA
"KINGSWOOD"

New coinage designs in the copper, copper-nickel, and silver series, as introduced during the 1851-1860 span. A display holder adds much to the appreciation of such a collection.

The 1856 Flying Eagle cent, actually a pattern, illustrating the style produced for circulation in 1857 and 1858. The reverse motif of an agricultural wreath is also to be found on gold dollars and $3 pieces of the 1854-1889 years.

to bullion by speculators, bankers, and others, while additional pieces were shipped to bullion markets overseas. In order to stanch the loss of circulating coinage, the official authorized weights for the half dime, dime, quarter, and half dollar were lowered in 1853. For example, the half dollar, previously weighing 206¼ grains (of an alloy composed of 90% silver and 10% copper) was reduced to 192 grains of the same alloy. To signify the new standard, small arrowheads were placed to the left and the right of the date numerals from 1853 through 1855. After 1855 the lower weights remained, but the arrowheads were removed. Quarters and half dollars of 1853 have an additional feature: rays surrounding the eagle on the reverse.

The San Francisco Mint opened for business in 1854. By the end of the decade, silver coins produced included dimes, quarters, half dollars, and one variety of silver dollar (1859-S).

The decade of the 1850s saw a great increase in the interest in coin collecting. Whereas in 1850 just a few dozen people at most were interested in the hobby, by 1860 enthusiasts numbered many hundreds. Doubtless, *The American Numismatical Manual*, a hefty book on coin collecting written by Professor Montroville W. Dickeson and published in 1859, helped to fan the flames of enthusiasm, as did the sale to the public for the first time of Proof coins in 1858, the setting up of several professional numismatic firms (coins were usually handled in addition to antiques and other artifacts in the early days), the conducting of several coin sales, and publicity and interest surrounding the gathering of specimens for the Mint Cabinet (which displayed the National Coin Collection; now on display at the Smithsonian Institution). The decade of the 1850s was one of enthusiasm on the American scene, with many advances being made in transportation, publishing, westward development, technology, and other fields. But, the clouds of war were gathering, and soon the Civil War embroiled the nation and pitted North against South, brother against brother.

A type set of copper, copper-nickel, and silver coins of the decade contains no major rarities, but specimens of certain issues in higher grades can be a challenge to locate.

CENT
1856-1858 Flying Eagle

Designed by: James Barton Longacre
Issue dates: 1856 (pattern issue)-1858
Composition: 0.88 part copper, 0.12 part nickel
Diameter: 19 mm
Weight: 72 grains
Edge: Plain
Business strike mintage: 42,050,000
Proof mintage: Fewer than 2,000

To create the Flying Eagle cent, Mint engraver James B. Longacre borrowed two motifs from the past. The obverse employs an eagle in flight, borrowed from Christian Gobrecht's silver dollar patterns of the 1836-1839 years. Above is the inscription UNITED STATES OF AMERICA, while the date is below. The reverse displays a wreath of cotton, corn, wheat, and tobacco enclosing the word ONE CENT, the wreath itself having been used earlier on Longacre's designs for the $1 and $3 gold coins of 1854. In 1856, approximately 600 pattern Flying Eagle cents were made for distribution to influential people to help secure approval of the design. Soon, the scarcity of the issue became known to collectors, and pieces were selling for $2 or more each (stated more sensationally, they were selling for 200 times face value). The Mint subsequently produced Proof restrikes to the extent of 1,000 or more coins, thus accounting for most Proof Flying Eagle cents known today (for relatively few Proofs were made in 1857 and 1858). In 1857, Flying Eagle cents were minted in large quantities for circulation. Coinage in large quantity for circulation continued through 1858. Trouble developed with the striking up of the design, as often the head, upper wing tip, and tail of the eagle would be weakly impressed. As a result, the motif was discontinued.

For a type set, no difficulty will be encountered in the search for an 1857 or 1858 Flying Eagle cent in any grade from Fine through Extremely Fine. AU pieces are not difficult to find, and Uncirculated coins appear with some frequency. Truly superb Uncirculated pieces are rare.

CENT
1859 Indian, Laurel Wreath

Designed by: James Barton Longacre
Issue date: 1859
Composition: 0.88 part copper, 0.12 part nickel
Diameter: 19 mm
Weight: 72 grains
Edge: Plain
Business strike mintage: 36,400,000
Proof mintage: 800 (estimated)

Following a pattern coinage in 1858, the Indian cent motif was used for circulating coinage in 1859, during which year 36,400,000 were struck. The obverse depicts a stylized Indian facing left, wearing a feathered headdress upon which is a band inscribed LIBERTY. To the left is UNITED STATES, and behind the head appears OF AMERICA. The date is below. The reverse employed on the 1859 cent shows a narrow wreath of laurel leaves enclosing the word ONE CENT. Although the laurel wreath was discontinued for cent coinage after 1859, Longacre brought it to life later for an adaptation used on the reverse of the nickel three-cent piece (minted 1865-1889).

Examples of the 1859 Indian cent are readily available in all grades from Good through AU. Uncirculated coins are scarcer, and superb Uncirculated pieces are quite elusive. Proofs were made for collectors, to the extent of an estimated 800 coins, and are occasionally available, although superb Proofs are decidedly rare.

CENT
1860-1864 Indian, Oak Wreath, Copper-Nickel

Designed by: James Barton Longacre
Issue dates: 1860-1864
Composition: 0.88 part copper, 0.12 part nickel
Diameter: 19 mm
Weight: 72 grains
Edge: Plain
Business strike mintage: 122,321,000
Proof mintage: Fewer than 2,500

Copper-nickel alloy (88% copper, 12% nickel) cents of the 1860-1864 years have a different reverse from the preceding and illustrate a broad wreath of oak leaves, surmounted with a shield, enclosing ONE CENT. The obverse Indian head motif remains the same as used in 1859. All throughout the Civil War these pieces were produced in large quantities, although hoarding by the public in 1863 withdrew most of them from circulation.

The numismatist today can easily acquire a representative 1860-1864 copper-nickel Indian cent in any grade from Good through AU, although 1861 is more expensive and is considered to be a slightly scarcer date. Uncirculated coins are scarce, and superb Uncirculated pieces are rare. Proofs are rare, with most of them showing some normal flecks or oxidation marks. Superb Proofs are extremely rare.

SILVER THREE-CENT PIECE
1851-1853 No Outline to Star

Designed by: James Barton Longacre
Issue dates: 1851-1853
Composition: 0.75 part silver, 0.25 part copper
Diameter: 14 mm
Weight: 12.35 grains (.8 gram)
Edge: Plain
Business strike mintage: 36,230,940
Proof mintage: Fewer than 60

The silver three-cent piece appeared in 1851 and was intended to facilitate the purchase of three-cent stamps at various post office outlets. The obverse of the 1851-1853 style bears a six pointed star at the center, upon which is a shield. UNITED STATES OF AMERICA and the date are around the border. The reverse employs a C-shaped ornament enclosing the Roman numeral III, with 13 stars surrounding. From the very outset, difficulties were experienced in striking the pieces up properly, with the result that many examples seen today are lightly impressed in one area or another or show adjustment marks (made at the Mint during the planchet preparation process). The small diameter of the coin evoked criticism. Although large quantities were produced during the early years of the series, particularly in 1852 and 1853, subsequent production declined, and the denomination never achieved widespread popularity.

With the exception of the 1851-O (New Orleans Mint) issue, the only branch mint issue of the denomination, all varieties of the 1851-1853 coinage are readily available in grades from Good through Extremely Fine. As noted earlier, sharply struck pieces are elusive. AU coins are scarce, Uncirculated pieces are scarcer, and superb Uncirculated coins are quite rare.

SILVER THREE-CENT PIECE
1854-1858, Three Outlines to Star

Designed by: James Barton Longacre
Issue dates: 1854-1858
Composition: 0.900 part silver, 0.100 part copper
Diameter: 14 mm
Weight: 11.57 grains (.75 gram)
Edge: Plain
Business strike mintage: 4,914,000
Proof mintage: Fewer than 300

In an effort to facilitate the striking up of design details, the obverse motif of the silver three-cent piece was modified in 1854 by the addition of three outlines to the star. The result was just the opposite of that intended, and pieces of the 1854-1858 years were more difficult to produce than ever. Examples seen today nearly always are weakly struck around the borders and in certain other areas as well. Indeed, the 1854-1858 silver three-cent piece is the most poorly struck of any design type of the mid 19th century.

There will be no difficulty acquiring an example of this issue in any grade desired from Good through Extremely Fine. AU coins are scarce, and Uncirculated pieces are rare. Superb Uncirculated pieces are very rare. Sharply struck coins are seldom met with. For all practical purposes, the numismatist should be satisfied with an example which shows some lightness of impression, particularly around the borders. The year 1855 is considered to be the scarcest in the range and, curiously, of the five dates of this type, the 1855 is the single date which is occasionally, very occasionally, seen with some semblance of sharp striking.

SILVER THREE-CENT PIECE
1859-1873 Two Outlines to Star

Designed by: James Barton Longacre
Issue dates: 1859-1 73
Composition: 0.900 part silver, 0.100 part copper
Diameter: 14 mm
Weight: 11.57 grains (0.75 gram)
Edge: Plain
Business strike mintage: 1,572,600
Proof mintage: 10,840

The silver three-cent piece was again modified in 1859. The three outlines to the obverse star were discontinued in favor of two outlines. At last, the problem of weak striking was solved, and from this point forward specimens were much more sharply struck than their predecessors. Still, occasional weak strikes persisted. Examples were produced in large quantities for circulation from 1859 through 1862, after which time the hoarding of silver pieces during the Civil War made additional coinage redundant. After the war ended, in 1865, quantities produced remained small, for the coin was never popular with the public. Although several thousand business strikes are listed for each of various years from 1865 onward, today specimens encountered of these particular years are apt to be Proofs. Uncirculated examples of coins dated from 1866 through 1872 are extreme rarities. Most "Uncirculated" pieces seen by the writer have been Proofs. The last year, 1873, saw mintage only of Proofs, to the extent of an estimated 600 pieces.

The collector desiring an example for a type set will have no difficulty acquiring a specimen dated in the 1859 to 1862 range in grades from Fine through Extremely Fine or AU. Uncirculated pieces occur with some frequency, although truly superb examples are elusive. When they do occur they are apt to be dated 1861 or 1862. Among higher grade pieces, most often seen are Proofs.

HALF DIME
1853-1855 Arrows at Date

Designed by: Christian Gobrecht
Issue dates: 1853-1855
Composition: 0.900 part silver, 0.100 part copper
Diameter: 15.5 mm
Weight: 19.2 grains
Edge: Reeded
Business strike mintage: 25,060,020
Proof mintage: Fewer than 150

In 1853 the Liberty Seated design was modified by the addition of tiny arrowheads to the left and right of the date, to signify a decrease in the authorized weight from 20.625 grains to 19.2 grains. These arrows remained in place through 1855, after which they were discontinued, although the reduced weight remained in effect for later years as well. The obverse depicts Liberty seated on a rock, holding in her left hand a liberty cap on a pole and with her right hand holding a shield. Stars are above, and the date, with an arrowhead on each side, is below. The reverse is the same as used earlier and consists of an open wreath enclosing HALF DIME with UNITED STATES OF AMERICA surrounding. As earlier silver half dimes (and other silver denominations) were being hoarded, the mint produced an unprecedented quantity of half dimes of the with-arrows style, with the figure for 1853 totaling 13,210,020 at the Philadelphia Mint, whereas the highest mintage for any earlier half dime date since the inception of the denomination was 2,760,000, or less than a quarter of this figure, back in 1835.

The numismatist will have no difficulty in acquiring an example of this design in any desired grade from Good through AU. Uncirculated pieces are elusive, and superb Uncirculated pieces are scarce. The tremendous demand for them on the part of type set collectors has resulted in the supply being widespread.

HALF DIME
1860-1873 Legend Obverse

Designed by: Christian Gobrecht
Issue dates: 1860-1873
Composition: 0,900 part silver, 0.100 part copper
Diameter: 15.5 mm.
Weight: 19.2 grains
Edge: Reeded
Business strike mintage: 15,552,600
Proof mintage: 10,040

In the half dime (and also the dime) series a modification to the design occurred in 1860. The Liberty Seated motif was retained as the central obverse design, but the peripheral stars were eliminated in favor of the inscription UNITED STATES OF AMERICA, which previously had appeared around the border of the reverse. The date remained below Liberty. The reverse wreath was restyled to a larger format without lettering at the border, enclosing the denomination expressed as HALF DIME. This style was continued through 1873, at which time the half dime denomination was terminated.

The type set collector will have no difficulty acquiring a commoner date in this era in any desired grade from Very Good to AU. Uncirculated pieces are harder to find, and superb Uncirculated half dimes are quite scarce. Proofs were issued to collectors and are generally available. Scattered among the common dates in the series are several scarce varieties, including several of the Philadelphia Mint issues.

DIME
1853-1855 Arrows at Date

Designed by: Christian Gobrecht
Issue dates: 1853-1855
Composition: 0.900 part silver, 0.100 part copper
Diameter: 17.9 mm.
Weight: 38.4 grains
Edge: Reeded
Business strike mintage: 21,493,010
Proof mintage: Fewer than 150

As a counter to widespread hoarding of silver coins in the early 1850s, when the silver in a dime (and other denominations) became worth more than the face value, the weight of a dime was reduced from 41.25 grains to 38.4 grains. To signify this change, tiny arrowheads were placed to the left and the right of the date. Otherwise the Liberty Seated design remains the same as used from 1838 through early 1853. Large quantities were produced of the 1853 with-arrows Philadelphia Mint issues; a coinage in excess of 12 million. Lesser quantities were made of other issues, Philadelphia and San Francisco pieces, through 1855.

The type set collector can easily acquire a specimen of this issue in any desired grade from Good through Extremely Fine or AU. Uncirculated pieces are scarce, and superb Uncirculated coins are quite difficult to find.

DIME
1860-1891 Legend Obverse

Designed by: Christian Gobrecht
Issue dates: 1860-1891
Composition: 0.900 part silver, 0.100 part copper
Diameter: 17.9 mm.
Weight: 38.4 grains 1860 to 1873 no arrows: 38.58 grains later
Edge: Reeded
Business strike mintage: 175,889,677
Proof mintage: 25,403

Like the half dime, the dime underwent a design change in 1860. The Liberty Seated motif was retained on the obverse, but the stars were removed, and in its place UNITED STATES OF AMERICA, formerly on the reverse, was inscribed. The date remained in its regular position below the base of Miss Liberty. The reverse wreath was restyled to a larger format enclosing the denomination expressed as ONE DIME. This style was produced continuously from 1860 through 1891. A number of scarce issues were made during that span, including Carson City pieces of the early 1870s. Dimes of 1873 and 1874 with arrows at the date constitute a separate type and are discussed in the following chapter.

Dimes of common dates in the 1860-1891 range are readily available in desired grades from Good through AU. Uncirculated pieces are not difficult to find, and superb Uncirculated coins are likewise available. Proofs were struck for collectors and are available for the various Philadelphia Mint issues. Of all Liberty Seated coins in the 1870s through the 1890s—dimes, quarters, half dollars—more dimes by far survive today than do quarters and half dollars.

QUARTER DOLLAR
1853 Arrows and Rays

Designed by: Christian Gobrecht
Issue date: 1853
Composition: 0.900 part silver, 0.10 part copper
Diameter: 24.3 mm.
Weight: 96 grains
Edge: Reeded
Business strike mintage: 16,542,000
Proof mintage: Fewer than 10

As also happened with the half dime and dime, quarter dollars were reduced in weight in 1853 as a measure against the hoarding and melting of newly released pieces. The authorized weight, previously 103.125 grains, was lowered to 96 grains. To signify this, arrows were placed to the left and the right of the date on the obverse, and rays were added above the eagle on the reverse. The rays were used only in 1853 and thus constitute a separate type. In 1854 (see following page) the rays were removed, thus creating the type with arrows at date and without rays on the reverse. Mintage was accomplished at the Philadelphia and New Orleans facilities, with 15,210,000 at the former location and 1,332,000 at the latter.

Numismatists will have no difficulty acquiring an example of the 1853 Philadelphia Mint issue in any desired grade from Good through Extremely Fine. AU pieces are scarcer, and Uncirculated coins are fairly elusive. Superb Uncirculated pieces are seldom met with.

QUARTER DOLLAR
1854-1855 Arrows Only

Designed by: Christian Gobrecht
Issue dates: 1854-1855
Composition: 0.900 part silver, 0.100 part copper
Diameter: 24.3 mm.
Weight: 96 grains
Edge: Reeded
Business strike mintage: 17,293,400
Proof mintage: Fewer than 140

The Liberty Seated quarter with arrows at date and rays on the reverse design was modified in 1854 by dropping the rays on the reverse but retaining the obverse arrows. Otherwise the type is essentially the same as produced from 1838 through early 1853. Coinage was effected at the Philadelphia, New Orleans, and San Francisco mints, the latter mint beginning production of the denomination in 1855. The most plentiful of the two 1854-1855 dates is 1854, of which 12,380,000 were produced, a figure which accounts for over half of the entire quantity of the type.

Specimens of the 1854, the most common date, are readily available in grades from Good through Extremely Fine. AU pieces are scarcer, and Uncirculated coins are fairly elusive. Superb Uncirculated pieces are rare.

HALF DOLLAR
1853 Arrows and Rays

Designed by: Christian Gobrecht
Issue date: 1853
Composition: 0.900 part silver, 0.100 part copper
Diameter: 30.6 mm.
Weight: 192 grains
Edge: Reeded
Business strike mintage: 4,860,708
Proof mintage: Fewer than 10

In 1853, when the authorized weight of the half dollar was reduced from 206.25 grains to 192 grains, the change was noted on the coins by the addition of small arrowheads to each side of the date and rays above the eagle on the reverse. Otherwise the Liberty Seated motif remained the same as used from 1839 onward. Just two varieties were produced: the 1853 Philadelphia issue of which 3,532,708 were made, and the 1853-O (New Orleans) with a mintage of 1,328,000.

Examples of the type are readily available in grades from Good through Extremely Fine or AU. Uncirculated coins are scarce, and truly superb Uncirculated pieces are rare.

HALF DOLLAR
1854-1855 Arrows Only

Designed by: Christian Gobrecht
Issue dates: 1854-1855
Composition: 0.900 part silver, 0.100 part copper
Diameter: 30.6 mm.
Weight: 192 grains
Edge: Reeded
Business strike mintage: 12,799,450
Proof mintage: Fewer than 140

The Liberty Seated half dollar style of 1854-1855 with arrowheads at the date is the same as used in 1853 except that the reverse rays have been deleted. Thus, 1854-1855 dollars stand as a distinct type. Coinage was produced primarily at Philadelphia and New Orleans. In 1855 the San Francisco Mint issued the denomination for the first time, striking 129,950 pieces. This remains the only rare mintmark variety in the date span. An interesting variation is provided by the 1855/4 overdate, a variety which exists in business strike form as well as Proof.

Examples of the 1854-1855 design are readily available in all grades from Good through Extremely Fine to AU. Uncirculated pieces are scarce, and superb Uncirculated pieces are scarcer yet, although they are not nearly so rare as comparable examples of the 1853 with arrows and rays style.

Chapter 6

New Issues
BRONZE, NICKEL, AND
SILVER 1861-1900

New designs which appeared during the 1861-1900 era include many interesting types, some of which were quite short lived, the 1883 without CENTS Liberty nickel being an example. The era itself was one of great change in America. At the outset the Civil War was raging, after which there were the unsettled conditions and turmoil of Reconstruction, followed by all sorts of shenanigans in the international gold market, the securities field, and banking. Silver was produced in vast quantities in Nevada in the 1860s and early 1870s, leading to the establishment of the Carson City Mint, which turned out its first coins in 1870. The market for silver bullion fell later in the decade, causing vested interests in the West to promote the Bland-Allison Act, which saw the production of hundreds of millions of unwanted and unneeded silver dollars of the new Morgan design. The situation had a beneficial effect on coin collecting decades later, when numismatists were delighted to find that countless Morgan dollars of earlier dates in Uncirculated grade could be obtained at face value or close to it. The Treasury release of silver dollars in quantity, which occurred in 1962 and 1963, set the stage for a tremendous increase in coin collecting. Morgan dollars, rather obscure at the time so far as collector interest was concerned, catapulted to the forefront, and by the 1970s and 1980s the series was probably number one in most collectors' minds. Then there were such coins as the two-cent piece, intended to be a convenience by substituting a single coin for two Indian cents. It didn't work out, and before long the denomination was discontinued. Related was the experience of the nickel three-cent piece, which was launched with great expectations in 1865. Almost from the very outset, mintage figures dropped sharply, and shortly more than a decade later, coinage was limited to just a few thousand pieces each year. The twenty-cent piece, of the Liberty Seated design and nearly the same diameter as the quarter dollar, was confusing to the public and saw one year of quantity production,

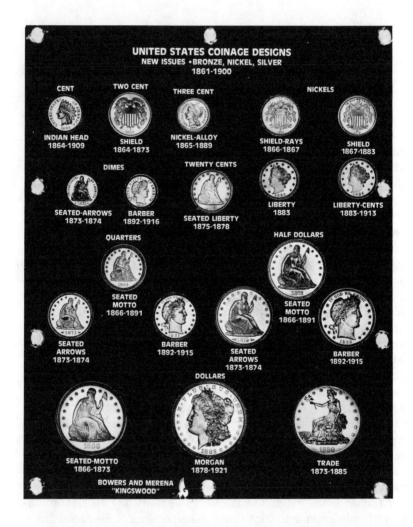

UNITED STATES COINAGE DESIGNS
NEW ISSUES •BRONZE, NICKEL, SILVER
1861-1900

CENT
INDIAN HEAD
1864-1909

TWO CENT
SHIELD
1864-1873

THREE CENT
NICKEL-ALLOY
1865-1889

NICKELS
SHIELD-RAYS
1866-1867

SHIELD
1867-1883

DIMES
SEATED-ARROWS
1873-1874

BARBER
1892-1916

TWENTY CENTS
SEATED LIBERTY
1875-1878

LIBERTY
1883

LIBERTY-CENTS
1883-1913

QUARTERS
SEATED
MOTTO
1866-1891

SEATED
ARROWS
1873-1874

BARBER
1892-1915

SEATED
ARROWS
1873-1874

HALF DOLLARS
SEATED
MOTTO
1866-1891

BARBER
1892-1915

DOLLARS
SEATED-MOTTO
1866-1873

MORGAN
1878-1921

TRADE
1873-1885

BOWERS AND MERENA
"KINGSWOOD"

A display of new bronze, nickel, and silver designs introduced during the 1851-1900 span. This period marked many significant changes in the coinage spectrum.

The two-cent piece made its debut in 1864 and was continued in production through 1873. The shield design on the obverse is related to that used on nickel five-cent pieces of the 1866-1883 span. Despite great expectations by the Treasury Department, two-cent pieces proved to be unpopular with the public and were soon discontinued.

Designed by Charles E. Barber, the Liberty Head or Barber half dollar made its debut in 1892 and was continued through 1915. Dimes and quarters featuring the same obverse motif were minted from 1892 through 1916. The Heraldic Eagle reverse, used on quarters and half dollars (but not dimes), is another adaptation of the Great Seal of the United States.

1875, followed by low mintages and then discontinuation.

In 1873 a new denomination, the trade dollar, appeared. Its intent was to serve in the Orient as a trading medium. Merchants in China preferred Mexican dollars, which were slightly heavier than the American standard of 412 grains. So, the trade dollar, weighing 420 grains, was created. After quantity production for a few years, the denomination was terminated. In the meantime, the authorized weights of certain silver coins were increased slightly. To signify this, arrowheads were placed near the dates of some 1873 and all 1874 dimes, quarters, and half dollars.

During the Civil War, agitation arose for the addition of a timely motto to our nation's coinage. Such ideas as GOD OUR TRUST and GOD AND COUNTRY were proposed, but finally adopted was IN GOD WE TRUST, taken from a stanza of the *Star Spangled Banner* which noted: "And let this be our motto: In God is our trust." The term first appeared on circulating coinage with the two-cent piece of 1864. Two years later, in 1866, IN GOD WE TRUST was added to the reverse of the quarter, half dollar, silver dollar, and large denomination gold coins. In later years the motto became a part of nearly every new coin design, unless space requirements prevented it.

The 1861-1900 era closed with the so-called Gay Nineties, an era remembered for its conviviality and good times. The Victorian period was drawing to a close, and the coming 20th century would bring with it changes no one had dreamed of earlier.

CENT
Indian Head 1864-1909, Bronze

Designed by: James B. Longacre
Issue dates: 1864-1909, bronze
Composition: Bronze (95% copper, 5% tin and zinc)
Diameter: 19 mm.
Weight: 48 grains
Edge: Plain
Business strike mintage: 1,690,839,942
Proof mintage: 98,000 (estimated)

The Indian head cent, designed by James B. Longacre and introduced into the coinage system in 1859, was struck in copper-nickel alloy (88% copper and 12% nickel) from that point through the middle òf the Civil War. During that conflict, coins of all types were hoarded, including copper-nickel cents. In their place appeared thousands of different varieties of privately-issued cent-size tokens struck in bronze. These were readily accepted by the public. The situation did not go unnoticed at the Mint, and soon a proposal was made to drop the copper-nickel metal, which had caused many striking difficulties due to its hardness, and replace it with bronze. This was done in 1864. Apart from the metallic composition, the format remained the same as used earlier. Later in 1864, a tiny L, the initial of Longacre, was added inconspicuously on the obverse. The position of the last feather of the headdress in relation to the last several letters of AMERICA was changed in 1886.

Although there are a number of scarce varieties within the 1864-1909 span, including 1864 with L on ribbon, 1871, 1872, 1877 (in particular), and 1909-S, there are enough common dates that obtaining a specimen in any desired condition presents no problem. Examples are easily available in grades from Good through Uncirculated, although pristine, superb Uncirculated pieces are becoming increasingly scarce. Proofs were made in fairly large quantities and are readily available, particularly of dates after 1877.

TWO-CENT PIECE
1864-1873

Designed by: James B. Longacre
Issue dates: 1864-1873
Composition: Bronze (95% copper, 5% tin and zinc)
Diameter: 23 mm.
Weight: 96 grains
Edge: Plain
Business strike mintage: 45,601,000
Proof mintage: 7,500 (estimated)

The two-cent piece, made in pattern form as early as 1836, was first used in circulation in 1864. The obverse design depicts a shield with two arrows behind, a wreath surrounding, and the motto IN GOD WE TRUST on a ribbon above. The date is near the bottom border. The reverse illustrates an open wreath enclosing the denomination 2 CENTS, with UNITED STATES OF AMERICA around the border. Intended to alleviate the coin shortage of the Civil War era and to provide for a convenient substitution for two individual cents, the two-cent piece was minted in large quantities during the first two years of its existence, after which the mintage figures declined, until in 1873 the mintage was limited just to Proofs for collectors.

Specimens of early years, particularly 1864 through 1869, are readily available in any grade desired from Good through AU. Uncirculated pieces are scarce, and superb Uncirculated pieces with full original mint color are quite elusive. Rarities in the series include the 1864 Small Motto, the 1869/8 overdate, and the Proof-only 1873.

NICKEL THREE-CENT PIECE
1865-1889

Designed by: James Barton Longacre
Issue dates: 1865-1889
Composition: 0.75 part copper and 0.25 part nickel, an alloy
  commonly called "nickel"
Diameter: 17.9 mm.
Weight: 29.94 grains (1.94 grams)
Edge: Plain
Business strike mintage: 31,332,527
Proof mintage: 56,000 (estimated)

Nickel three-cent pieces were intended to serve as small change
in circulation and as a substitute for the silver three-cent pieces, in
an era in which the government was releasing little new silver coinage into circulation. Silver coin shipments were suspended during
the Civil War and were not fully resumed until the early 1870s. Despite great expectations, as evidenced by a mintage of over 11 million the first year, the pieces were not well accepted, and from that
point the mintages declined. In later years very few were struck. The
obverse design consists of Miss Liberty wearing a diadem inscribed
LIBERTY, her hair neatly arranged. UNITED STATES OF AMERI-
CA and the date surround. The reverse is an adaptation of the laurel wreath earlier used on the 1859 Indian cent, enclosing the Roman numeral III.

Numismatists desiring circulated examples of the nickel three-cent
piece will find that coins from Good through AU grades are readily
available for most issues of the decade beginning with the 1865 date.
Uncirculated coins are also seen with regularity, although truly superb pieces are scarce. Those desiring Proofs will have a better selec-
tion among later issues, which were produced in large quantities.
Business strikes are apt to be lightly impressed in areas, a result of
the hard nickel alloy not completely filling all of the recesses in the
dies.

NICKEL FIVE-CENT PIECE
1866-1867 Shield, Rays on Reverse

Designed by: James B. Longacre
Issue dates: 1866-1867
Composition: 75% copper, 25% nickel
Diameter: 20.5 mm.
Weight: 77.16 grains (5 grams)
Edge: Plain
Business strike mintage: 16,761,500
Proof mintage: 500 (estimated)

The nickel-five cent piece made its appearance in 1866 as a substitute for the half dime, for the Treasury Department at the time was withholding silver coins from circulation. The first design was the Shield style with rays on the obverse. The obverse closely follows the design of the two-cent piece and consists of a shield with a wreath surrounding the upper portion, a cross at the top, and two crossed arrows at the bottom. IN GOD WE TRUST is above, and the date is below. The reverse is dominated by the central numeral 5, from which emanate 13 rays interspersed among as many stars. The inscription UNITED STATES OF AMERICA and CENTS appears around the border. It was quickly learned that the hard nickel alloy plus the features of the design caused coins to strike up lightly, with many design details often weak or missing. It was believed that the elimination of rays from the reverse would simplify the design and reduce metal movement in the die, thus solving the problem. Accordingly, the rays were discontinued early in 1867.

Examples of the 1866-1867 Shield nickel with rays are readily available in grades from Good through AU. Uncirculated pieces are scarce, and truly superb Uncirculated coins are rare. A number of Proofs were minted for collectors, particularly in 1866, when it is believed that nearly 500 were made. The 1867 with rays is scarcer in all grades, and in Proof it is a major rarity.

NICKEL FIVE-CENT PIECE
1867-1883 Shield, Without Rays

Designed by: James Barton Longacre
Issue dates: 1867-1883
Composition: 75% copper, 25% nickel
Diameter: 20.5 mm.
Weight: 77.16 grains (5 grams)
Edge: Plain
Business strike mintage: 111,256,110
Proof mintage: 31,000 (estimated)

The Shield nickel style of 1867-1883 is similar to that of 1866 except that the 13 rays between the stars on the reverse have been eliminated. This alleviated the problem of weak striking to an extent, with the result that Shield nickels of this type are generally better struck than earlier pieces, although the majority of surviving coins show weakness in one area or another. Die breakage was a common occurrence, and often inspection with a magnifying glass will reward the viewer with a glimpse of a myriad of tiny cracks, which lend interest to a coin. From 1867 through 1883 coinage was continuous, although in 1877 and 1878 no business strikes were produced; the issues of those two years were limited to Proofs for collectors.

Numismatists will have no difficulty obtaining a common date such as most years from 1867 through 1876, and also 1882 and 1883, in any grade desired from Good through AU. Uncirculated pieces are scarce and superb Uncirculated pieces are rare. Proofs were made in fairly large numbers for collectors and are readily available, although most uncleaned examples show light flecks or spots as a result of moisture over the years.

NICKEL FIVE-CENT PIECE
1883 Liberty, Without CENTS

Designed by: Charles E. Barber
Issue date: 1883
Composition: 75% copper, 25% nickel
Diameter: 21.2 mm.
Weight: 77.16 grains (5 grams)
Edge: Plain
Business strike mintage: 5,474,000
Proof mintage: 5,219

In 1883 a new design appeared, the Liberty Head motif by Charles E. Barber. The obverse depicts the head of Miss Liberty, perhaps modeled after the goddess Diana, wearing a coronet inscribed LIBERTY and surrounded by 13 stars, with the date below. The reverse shows an agricultural wreath, open at the top, enclosing the Roman letter V as the only mark of value. UNITED STATES OF AMERICA and the motto E PLURIBUS UNUM surround. The word CENTS does not appear on the coin. Unscrupulous persons gold-plated the pieces and passed them off as $5 gold coins to unsuspecting merchants and citizens. The mint realized that a design error had been created, and soon the word CENTS was added to the reverse (see next listing). In the meantime, the variety captured the fancy of the public, and rumors quickly spread that the mint was calling them in (not true) and that the value would soon rise sharply. As a result, vast quantities were hoarded. Collectors joined the game, and many Proofs were ordered, resulting in a nearly record mintage of 5,219 Proof examples.

In grades from Good through Uncirculated, particularly in higher grades from Extremely Fine through AU, examples are easily available. Superb Uncirculated coins are also available, but some searching may be required to locate a nice one. Proofs are often seen, as the generous mintage would indicate.

NICKEL FIVE-CENT PIECE
1883-1913 Liberty, With CENTS

Designed by: Charles E. Barber
Issue dates: 1883-1913
Composition: 75% copper, 25% nickel
Diameter: 21.2 mm.
Weight: 77.16 grains (5 grams)
Edge: Plain
Business strike mintage: 596,535,965
Proof mintage: 79,923

Following the introduction of the Liberty nickel without CENTS, the omission of this key word was realized, and the reverse design was modified to incorporate CENTS below the wreath. The motto E PLURIBUS UNUM, earlier in that space, was reduced in size and placed in an arc above the wreath. This style was continued through the end of the series in 1912. Coinage was continuous from 1883 onward. Scarce early dates include 1885 (the key issue) and 1886. In 1912, nickel five-cent pieces were struck at branch mints for the first time; at Denver and San Francisco. Sometime after 1912, some 1913-dated Liberty Head nickels were struck. The quantity was not recorded, but only five such pieces are known to collectors today.

The numismatist seeking an example for a type set will have no difficulty acquiring a common date, particularly in the 1900-1912 span, in any grade desired from Good through AU. Uncirculated pieces are scarcer, and superb Uncirculated pieces are quite elusive. Many Liberty nickels show evidence of light striking on certain of the obverse stars and also on the reverse wreath, particularly in the lower portion at the left. It may take some searching to find a sharply struck example. Proofs, which were made in fairly large quantities throughout the series, usually are sharply struck and can be obtained without difficulty, although uncleaned pieces often show light flecks due to moisture.

DIME
1873-1874 With Arrows

Designed by: Christian Gobrecht
Issue dates: 1873-1874
Composition: 0.900 part silver, 0.100 part copper
Diameter: 17.9 mm.
Weight: 38.58 grains (2.50 grams)
Edge: Reeded
Business strike mintage: 6,041,608
Proof mintage: 1,500

In 1873 the authorized weight of the dime was raised slightly from 38.4 grains to 38.58 grains, the latter figure precisely equaling 2.50 grams. To signify the change, small arrowheads were placed to the left and the right of the date on the dime (and also the quarter and half dollar). Dimes minted in 1873 before the change was made are without arrows. The with-arrows format was employed in the latter part of 1873 as well as all of 1874. After that time the weight remained the same, but the arrows were discontinued. The design otherwise remains the same, with Liberty seated on the obverse and a wreath motif on the reverse.

Sufficient quantities of business strikes were made that the numismatist should encounter no problem finding coins in any desired grade from Good through Extremely Fine to AU. Uncirculated pieces are elusive, and superb Uncirculated coins are even more difficult to locate. Survivors of the Proof mintage, totaling 1,500 coins for the two years, can be found, although superb pieces are rare. Within the business strike mintage there are two scarce varieties, the Carson City issues: 1873-CC and 1874-CC.

DIME
1892-1916 Barber

Designed by: Charles E. Barber
Issue dates: 1892-1916
Composition: 0.900 part silver, 0.100 part copper
Diameter: 17.9 mm.
Weight: 38.58 grains
Edge: Reeded
Business strike mintage: 504,317,075
Proof mintage: 17,353

In 1892 the dime, quarter, and half dollar denominations were redesigned. A Liberty Head motif common to all three denominations made its appearance the same year. Known as the Barber dime, the ten-cent denomination featured on the obverse Miss Liberty facing right, her hair in a Phrygian cap and wearing a laurel wreath, with the word LIBERTY in tiny letters in a band above her forehead. The inscription UNITED STATES OF AMERICA surrounds, and the date is below. The reverse is of the same design used earlier and features a large wreath enclosing ONE DIME. There was no room for the motto IN GOD WE TRUST on the coin, so it was omitted. It is not generally realized that the obverse design of the dime differs from that of the quarter and half dollar, in that the latter denominations have stars around the obverse periphery.

While there are a number of scarcities and rarities in the 1892-1916 series, the exceedingly rare 1894-S dime being famous among them, there are enough common dates that the type set collector will encounter no difficulty acquiring an example in any desired grade from Good through AU. Uncirculated pieces are elusive, although hardly rare, while superb Uncirculated coins are more difficult to find. Proofs were minted each year from 1892 to 1915 (but not 1916) for collectors, and these can be obtained with some searching.

TWENTY-CENT PIECE
1875-1878 Liberty Seated

Designed by: William Barber (obverse after Christian Gobrecht)
Issue dates: 1875-1878
Composition: 0.900 part silver, 0.100 part copper
Diameter: 22 mm.
Weight: 77.16 grains
Edge: Plain
Business strike mintage: 1,349,840
Proof mintage: 5,000

The Act of March 3, 1875 authorized the twenty-cent piece. It was felt that the denomination would find an enthusiastic reception in the West, but it was soon learned that the public confused the pieces with quarter dollars of approximately the same diameter. The obverse design features Christian Gobrecht's motif of Miss Liberty seated, stars surrounding, and the date below. The reverse is a new motif by William Barber and depicts a perched eagle, somewhat similar in configuration to that used on the trade dollar, surrounded by UNITED STATES OF AMERICA and the denomination expressed as TWENTY CENTS. The edge is plain, unlike other silver denominations of the era.

The type set collector will gravitate toward an example of 1875-S, the issue which is most often seen. Specimens are readily available in grades from Very Good to Extremely Fine. AU pieces are scarce, and Uncirculated coins are quite elusive. Truly superb Uncirculated pieces are rare. The striking is apt to be erratic, and often pieces will show lightness of impression, particularly on the eagle on the reverse and on the Liberty Seated figure and stars on the obverse. Many Philadelphia Mint business strike coins in higher grades exhibit prooflike surfaces. Proofs are available of the four Philadelphia issues 1875 through 1878.

QUARTER DOLLAR
1866-1891 With Motto

Designed by: Christian Gobrecht
Issue dates: 1866-1891
Composition: 0.900 part silver, 0.100 part copper
Diameter: 24.3 mm.
Weight: 96 grains 1866 to 1873 no arrows; 96.45 grains later
Edge: Reeded
Business strike mintage: 72,680,181
Proof mintage: 20,923

In 1866 the motto IN GOD WE TRUST was added to the reverse of the Liberty Seated quarter dollar, half dollar, and silver dollar. The Liberty Seated obverse in combination with the eagle reverse with added motto was continued in use through 1891. A distinctly different type is represented by certain issues of 1873 and all quarter dollars of 1874 with arrows at the date (as discussed in the next listing). Mintage was continuous from 1866 through 1891 at the Philadelphia Mint. In addition, the San Francisco and Carson City mints produced many coins. The only New Orleans issue of the type is the 1891-O, made during the last year the design was in use. There are a number of rarities within the span, with top honors being held by the 1873-CC (variety without arrows at date) of which just two specimens are known to exist.

The type set collector will have no difficulty acquiring an example of one of the common dates in this span in grades from Good through Very Fine or so, although it is the case that Liberty Seated quarters of this era are much scarcer than contemporary dimes and are slightly scarcer than half dollars. Extremely Fine pieces can be found with some searching, AU coins are scarcer, Uncirculated pieces are scarcer yet, and superb Uncirculated pieces are rare. Proofs are available in proportion to the original mintages.

QUARTER DOLLAR
1873-1874 With Arrows

Designed by: Christian Gobrecht
Issue dates: 1873-1874
Composition: 0.900 part silver, 0.100 part copper
Diameter: 24.3 mm.
Weight: 96.45 grains (6.25 grams)
Edge: Reeded
Business strike mintage: 2,302,822
Proof mintage: 1,240

In 1873 the authorized weight of the quarter dollar was raised from 96 grains to 96.45 grains, the latter figure equaling 6.25 grams. To signify the new standard, arrows were added to the date of quarter dollars produced later in 1873 and all quarter dollars produced in 1874. After 1874 the weight remained the same, but the arrows were no longer used. Otherwise, the Liberty Seated design, with the motto IN GOD WE TRUST on the reverse, is the same as that used from 1866 through 1891.

Examples of this type are readily available in grades from Good through Fine, although specimens are considerably scarcer than the related dimes of the same years. Very Fine pieces are scarce, Extremely Fine coins are quite scarce, AU pieces are rare, Uncirculated pieces are rarer yet, and superb Uncirculated pieces are very rare. Proofs are encountered now and then, in keeping with their original mintages. Among business strikes, there is one rarity, the 1873-CC, which is elusive in all grades.

QUARTER DOLLAR
1892-1916 Barber

Designed by: Charles E. Barber
Issue dates: 1892-1916
Composition: 0.900 part silver, 0.100 part copper
Diameter: 24.3 mm.
Weight: 96.45 grains
Edge: Reeded
Business strike mintage: 264,670,880
Proof mintage: 17,299

Charles E. Barber's Liberty Head motif, commonly referred to as the "Barber" style, was used on quarter dollars from 1892 through 1916. The obverse motif of Miss Liberty is similar to that found on the dime and half dollar and features her facing to the right, her hair in a Phrygian cap, wearing a laurel wreath, with LIBERTY on a small band above her forehead. Six stars are to the left and seven to the right, IN GOD WE TRUST is above, and the date is below. The reverse is an adaptation of the Great Seal of the United States and depicts a heraldic eagle holding in its talons an olive branch and arrows, although the branch and arrows are transposed from the position used on quarter (and other silver and gold) coinage nearly a century earlier. Above the eagle is a galaxy of 13 stars. UNITED STATES OF AMERICA and QUARTER DOLLAR surround.

For type set purposes, the numismatist will have no trouble finding coins from Good through Fine. Very Fine coins are scarce, and Extremely Fine pieces are quite scarce, at least in the context of more recent issues. AU and Uncirculated pieces are scarcer yet, and superb Uncirculated coins are rare. Proofs were produced of all years from 1892 through 1915 (but not 1916) and are available in proportion to their original mintage.

HALF DOLLAR
1866-1891 With Motto

Designed by: Christian Gobrecht
Issue dates: 1866-1891
Composition: 0.900 part silver, 0.100 part copper
Diameter: 30.6 mm.
Weight: 192 grains 1866 to 1873 no arrows; 192.9 grains later
Edge: Reeded
Business strike mintage: 56,138,834
Proof mintage: 20,923

The regular Liberty Seated design, which had been in use since 1839, was modified in 1866 by the addition of IN GOD WE TRUST to the reverse. The motto appears on a scroll or ribbon above the eagle. A similar change was effected in the quarter and dollar denominations. Production was continuous at the Philadelphia Mint from 1866 onward. Business strikes were also made at San Francisco and Carson City, with several of the Carson City varieties, particularly those in the early 1870s, being rare today. Certain half dollars of 1873 and all of 1874 have arrows at the date and are a separate type discussed in the next listing. Business strike Philadelphia Mint issues from 1879 through 1890 were produced in low numbers, as the Mint was busy turning out unprecedented quantities of silver dollars at the time.

Examples of common dates within the series, Philadelphia Mint issues of 1875 through 1878, for example, are relatively easy to obtain in grades from Good through Very Fine. Extremely Fine coins are scarcer, AU pieces are scarcer yet, and Uncirculated coins can be called very scarce. Superb Uncirculated pieces are quite rare. Proofs exist in proportion to their original mintages.

HALF DOLLAR
1873-1874 With Arrows

Designed by: Christian Gobrecht
Issue dates: 1873-1874
Composition: 0.900 part silver, 0.100 part copper
Diameter: 30.6 mm.
Weight: 192.9 grains (12.50 grams)
Edge: Reeded
Business strike mintage: 5,070,310
Proof mintage: 1,250

Part way through 1873 the authorized weight of the half dollar denomination was increased slightly from 192 grains to 192.9 grains, the latter equaling precisely 12.50 grams. To signify this change, arrowheads were placed to the left and right of the date. After 1874 the weight standard remained the same, but the arrows were no longer used. Otherwise, the Liberty Seated with IN GOD WE TRUST motto type is the same as that used from 1866 through 1891 inclusive.

The Philadelphia Mint produced the greatest number of coins during the 1873-1874 years, so the type set collector normally gravitates toward one of these. Examples are readily available in grades from Good through Very Fine, are quite scarce in Extremely Fine grade, are scarcer yet in AU preservation, and are rare in Uncirculated state. Superb Uncirculated pieces are very rare. Proofs exist in proportion to the original mintages. One rare business strike exists in the series: the 1874-CC, of which just 59,000 were minted.

HALF DOLLAR
1892-1915 Barber

Designed by: Charles E. Barber
Issue dates: 1892-1915
Composition: 0.900 part silver, 0.100 part copper
Diameter: 30.6 mm.
Weight: 192.9 grains
Edge: Reeded
Business strike mintage: 135,916,889
Proof mintage: 17,313

In 1892 the half dollar was redesigned to the so-called Barber type. Designer Charles E. Barber's Miss Liberty now faces right, her hair is in a Phrygian cap, and a wreath of laurel encircles her head. The word LIBERTY appears on a small band or ribbon above her forehead. IN GOD WE TRUST is above, six stars are to the left, seven stars are to the right, and the date is below. The reverse is an adaptation of the Great Seal of the United States and features a heraldic eagle grasping an olive branch and arrows and holding in its beak a ribbon inscribed E PLURIBUS UNUM. A galaxy of stars is above. UNITED STATES OF AMERICA and HALF DOLLAR surround. The same head of Miss Liberty appears on dimes and quarters of the era. Mintage was continuous at the Philadelphia and San Francisco Mints from 1892 through 1915, with additional pieces being supplied for many years by New Orleans and Denver.

The type set collector will encounter no difficulty in acquiring specimens in grades of Good or Very Good. Fine pieces, believe it or not, are scarce, Very Fine coins are very scarce, and Extremely Fine coins can be called rare in the context of modern issues. AU coins are rarer yet, Uncirculated pieces are still more rare, and superb Uncirculated pieces are very rare. Proofs exist in proportion to their original mintages. The reason for the rarity of higher grade circulated pieces is that, like quarter dollars of the same type, the word LIBERTY tended to wear quickly once pieces were placed in circulation.

SILVER DOLLAR
1866-1873 With Motto

Designed by: Christian Gobrecht
Issue dates: 1866-1873
Composition: 0.900 part silver, 0.100 part copper
Diameter: 38.1 mm.
Weight: 412.5 grains
Edge: Reeded
Business strike mintage: 3,597,888
Proof mintage: 6,060

The Liberty Seated dollar design was modified in 1866 by the addition of the motto IN GOD WE TRUST on the ribbon or scroll above the eagle on the reverse. Otherwise the design is essentially the same as that used from 1840 onward. The with-motto format continued in use through 1873. The glory days of the silver dollar denomination were yet to come, and mintages were low in comparison to what would happen with the Morgan silver dollar beginning in 1878. The only "common" Liberty Seated dollars in this range are the 1871 and 1872, and even they are scarce in relation to later issues.

As Liberty Seated silver dollars did not circulate as actively as smaller denominations, pieces in well-worn grades such as Good and Very Good are much scarcer (though no more desirable or expensive) than coins in Fine to Very Fine grade, the latter being the conditions typically seen. Extremely Fine pieces are available, AU coins are scarce, and Uncirculated pieces are scarcer yet. Superb Uncirculated coins are rarities. Proofs were made of all Philadelphia Mint issues and exist today in proportion to their original mintages.

SILVER DOLLAR
1878-1921 Morgan

Designed by: George T. Morgan
Issue dates: 1878-1921
Composition: 0.900 part silver, 0.100 part copper
Diameter: 38.1 mm.
Weight: 412.5 grains
Edge: Reeded
Business strike mintage: 656,989,387
Proof mintage: 23,723

In 1878 the passage of the Bland-Allison Act caused the eventual mintage of hundreds of millions of silver dollars. The Philadelphia Mint enlisted George T. Morgan to produce a new design. The obverse depicts Miss Liberty facing left, her hair in a Phrygian cap, and with LIBERTY inscribed on a ribbon or band holding a spray of leaves and sheaves. E PLURIBUS UNUM is above, seven stars are to the left, six stars are to the right, and the date is below. The reverse depicts a wingspread eagle holding a branch and three arrows. IN GOD WE TRUST appears in Old English letters above. Surrounding is the inscription UNITED STATES OF AMERICA and ONE DOLLAR. Production was continuous at the Philadelphia Mint from 1878 through 1904, after which there was a pause until the single year 1921. Additional pieces were made at San Francisco, Carson City, and New Orleans during the 1878-1904 span and in 1921 at Denver and San Francisco.

The type set collector will have no difficulty acquiring a common date Morgan dollar in any grade desired from Good through superb Uncirculated. Proofs were minted for all dates at Philadelphia, and their survival today is proportional to the original figures.

TRADE DOLLAR
1873-1885

Designed by: William Barber
Issue dates: 1873-1885
Composition: 0.900 part silver, 0.100 part copper
Diameter: 38.1 mm
Weight: 420 grains
Edge: Reeded
Business strike mintage: 35,954,535
Proof mintage: 11,404

The trade dollar was first minted in 1873 in response to the need for a coin to compete with the Mexican "dollar" in the Orient. Weighing 420 grains, or slightly heavier than a standard silver dollar, the trade dollar was intended for export only. The obverse depicts Miss Liberty seated on a bale, of merchandise, her right hand holding a branch, her left hand holding a ribbon inscribed LIBERTY, a sheaf of wheat behind, and the sea in front. IN GOD WE TRUST appears at the bottom just above the date. Stars surround the upper portion. The reverse depicts an eagle holding three arrows and a branch, with E PLURIBUS UNUM on a ribbon above, 420 GRAINS, 900 FINE. below. The inscription UNITED STATES OF AMERICA and TRADE DOLLAR surrounds.

The numismatist today can readily secure a trade dollar in grades from Fine through AU. Some pieces have chopmarks consisting of Oriental characters impressed by bankers and merchants when the pieces circulated in the Orient. Uncirculated coins are scarce, and superb Uncirculated pieces are rare. Proofs exist in proportion to their original mintages and are primarily available from the years from 1879 through 1883.

Chapter 7

New Issues
COPPER, NICKEL, AND
SILVER 1901-1950

The first part of the present century saw many different coinage designs appear, including the Lincoln cent, which subsequently went through several evolutions, the Buffalo and Jefferson nickels, and the beautiful new silver coinage designs which made their debut in 1916—the Mercury dime, Standing Liberty quarter dollar, and Walking Liberty half dollar. In the silver dollar series, the Peace design was first minted in 1921.

With the possible exception of the Peace silver dollar, which never did circulate widely in the channels of commerce (most were kept stored in banks), all of the issues in this set are familiar to my older readers, for examples were readily available in circulation in the 1950s and early 1960s.

Whereas 19th century coinage featured heraldic emblems, Miss Liberty in various stylistic forms, and other patriotic or allegorical motifs, coinage of the early 20th century began to emphasize actual people. President Lincoln appeared on the cent of 1909, Washington on the quarter of 1932, Jefferson on the nickel of 1938, Franklin Roosevelt on the dime of 1946, and a non-president, Benjamin Franklin, on the half dollar of 1948. The Buffalo or Indian head nickel, representing the native American race, fits in with the "real people" theme.

After the advent of depicting actual personalities in coins, the idea of romantic stylized figures was not dead. Indeed, in 1916 it may have reached its highest form in American silver coinage; at least that is the opinion of numerous collectors today. In that year, artists competed to produce new versions of the dime, quarter, and half dollar to replace the familiar Barber motif, which had been in use since 1892. Adolph Weinman's so-called "Mercury" dime and his Walking Liberty half dollar met with an enthusiastic acclaim, as did Hermon MacNeil's Standing Liberty quarter dollar.

Somewhat sadly for the sake of tradition, the new issues introduced during the 1901-1950 era marked the end of silver in our cir

Considered by numismatists to be a highlight among American coinage designs, the Standing Liberty motif, by Hermon A. MacNeil, appeared in 1916. This scantily-clad version of Miss Liberty caused a furor,
and in 1917 the design was revised by encasing her in a suit of armor!

Adolph A. Weinman, designer of the Liberty Head or "Mercury" dime shown above, a style minted from 1916 through 1945, also produced the illustrious Liberty Walking half dollar (minted from 1916 through 1947).

culating coinage. By 1964 the price of silver bullion had climbed to the point at which coins were worth more melted down than they were if spent at face value, essentially a rerun of the situation back in 1852-1853. Thus, the death knell of silver in circulating coinage was sounded.

Containing no great rarities, a type set consisting of new issues of the 1901-1950 era can be assembled without undue difficulty, although within the context of the set the 1916-1917 Type I Standing Liberty quarter is scarce.

CENT
1909 V.D.B. Lincoln

Designed by: Victor David Brenner
Issue date: 1909
Composition: Bronze (0.95 part copper, 0.05 part tin and zinc)
Diameter: 19 mm
Weight: 48 grains
Edge: Plain
Business strike mintage: 28,479,000
Proof mintage: 420

After several decades of use, the Indian motif, which had been a familiar sight on cents since 1859, was replaced by a new style, the Lincoln cent. Designed by noted sculptor Victor David Brenner, who earlier had modeled the bust of Lincoln for several medals and plaques, the new design depicted on the obverse a head and shoulders portrait of Lincoln, bearded, facing right. IN GOD WE TRUST is above, LIBERTY is to the left, and the date is at the lower right. The reverse consists of two wheat stalks, one to the left and the other to the right, enclosing ONE CENT and UNITED STATES OF AMERICA, with E PLURIBUS UNUM above. Significantly, on the 1909 issue the initials of the designer, V.D.B., appear prominently on the bottom of the reverse, centered below the wheat stalks. A few people complained about the prominence of Brenner's initials on the cent. The opposing voices were heard at the Mint, and soon the reverse was redesigned, and the offending V.D.B. initials were removed.

1909 V.D.B. cents, the Philadelphia Mint issue, are plentiful today in all grades from Good through Uncirculated, with most being in various worn conditions. Matte Proofs were minted to the extent of 420 pieces, but most of these were "spent," for collectors preferred the earlier mirrorlike style to the matte finish. Such Matte Proofs are extremely rare today. Note, however, that there is very little difference between a sharp business strike and a Matte Proof, and if you buy a Matte Proof, be sure it comes from an expert source.

CENT
1909-1958 Lincoln, Wreath Reverse

Designed by: Victor David Brenner
Issue dates: 1909-1958
Composition: Bronze (1909-1942), new alloy of 0.95 part copper
   and 0.05 zinc (1947-1958)
Diameter: 19 mm
Weight: 48 grains
Edge: Plain
Business strike mintage: 19,552,500,823
Proof mintage: 15,314 matte; 3,836,869 mirrorlike finish

After a brief coinage of Lincoln cents with V.D.B. initials on the
reverse, the initials were removed, thus creating the "wreath reverse,"
without initials, a style which remained in use through 1958. From
1909 through 1942, and again from 1948 through 1958, pieces were
struck in the standard bronze alloy consisting of 0.95 part copper
and 0.5 part tin and zinc. Separate types were created in 1943 with
the zinc-coated steel and in 1944-1946 with a special alloy made from
melted-down cartridge cases and which consisted of 0.95 part copper and 0.05 zinc; these last two types are discussed on following
separate pages. It should be noted that the V.D.B. initials were put
back on the Lincoln cent beginning in 1918, but this time they were
of minute size and placed on Lincoln's shoulder. Generally, collectors do not consider the types with shoulder initials and without
shoulder initials, or before 1918, and later, to be distinct types, although in a way they are.

Coined by the billions, cents of this type are common today, and
no difficulty will be encountered in obtaining one in any grade
desired from Good through superb Uncirculated, with the latter
grade being the obvious choice. In addition, Matte Proofs are available from the 1909-1916 years and brilliant-finish Proofs are available of the 1936-1942 years and again from 1950 through 1958. Today,
superb Matte Proofs are rare, while mirrorlike or brilliant Proofs of
the later era are readily obtained.

CENT
1943 Lincoln, Steel

Designed by: Victor David Brenner
Issue date: 1943
Composition: Zinc-coated steel
Diameter: 19 mm
Weight: 41.67 grains
Edge: Plain
Business strike mintage: 1,093,838,670
Proof mintage: None

During the early years of World War II copper was in short supply. In 1942 the Mint sought to replace copper in our coinage, and the Durez Chemical Company, North Tonawanda, New York, was commissioned to find substitutes. Experiments ensued, and medalets the approximate size of a cent were struck in such diverse materials as fibre, white metal, plastic, and zinc-coated steel. The last format was adopted, and the following year, 1943, saw the production of Lincoln cents in zinc-coated steel at the Philadelphia, Denver and San Francisco mints.

Examples of the 1943 Lincoln cent are readily available in all grades from Very Fine through superb Uncirculated, although worn grades tend to be a bit "scruffy" in appearance.

CENT
1944-1946 Lincoln, Shell Case Alloy

Designed by: Victor David Brenner
Issue dates: 1944-1946
Composition: Cartridge alloy (see note)
Diameter: 19 mm
Weight: 48 grains
Edge: Plain
Business strike mintage: 5,142,736,000
Proof mintage: None

Cartridge cases from spent ammunition used in the war effort were melted down and used as an alloy for Lincoln cents from 1944 through 1946. The change was scarcely noticeable. Coinage was effected in large quantities, with over one *billion* being coined in each of the years 1944 and 1945 at the Philadelphia Mint, an unprecedented figure representing the first time the billion mark had been crossed. Interestingly, by 20 years later multi-billion coinages were the rule.

Examples are readily available today in any desired grade from well-worn to superb Uncirculated. The coin will present no difficulty in acquisition.

Note: The exact metallic composition of cents made from cartridge alloy has not been determined by present day numismatists. These cartridge cased cents were the subject of an article by Ed Rochette in his "Coin Roundup" column released on July 31, 1983.

NICKEL FIVE-CENT PIECE
1913 Buffalo or Indian, Type I

Designed by: James E. Fraser
Issue date: 1913
Composition: 0.75 part copper, 0.25 part nickel
Diameter: 21.2 mm
Weight: 77.16 grains (5 grams)
Edge: Plain
Business strike mintage: 38,434,270
Proof mintage: 1,250

In 1913 the Liberty Head nickel, which had remained in service since 1883, was replaced by a new design, the so-called Buffalo (more properly, the Indian) nickel by James E. Fraser, a well-known sculptor. The obverse portrait was modeled from life by studying three Indian models, while the reverse was styled from a bison, popularly called a "buffalo," at the Bronx Zoo. The obverse depicts the head of an Indian facing right, with LIBERTY in small letters at the upper right edge, and the date at the lower left. The reverse shows a bison standing on a raised mound, UNITED STATES OF AMERICA and E PLURIBUS UNUM above, and FIVE CENTS on a mound below. It was found that the relief of the mound caused the inscription in that area to wear quickly, so the bottom part of the reverse was subsequently redesigned, creating the so-called Type II. The Type I is distinguished by the presence of a mound with FIVE CENTS inscribed on it, as noted. Production of business strikes was accomplished at Philadelphia, Denver, and San Francisco, with Philadelphia registering by far the largest mintage. At Philadelphia, 1,250 Matte Proof examples were made for collectors.

Examples of the 1913 Type I Buffalo nickel are readily available in all grades from About Good to Uncirculated. Superb Uncirculated coins are scarce, although not rare. Matte Proofs have survived in relatively few numbers, and of the 1,250 minted, probably not more than a few hundred still exist. As certain business strikes closely resemble Matte Proofs, care is to be taken when buying one of these.

NICKEL FIVE-CENT PIECE
1913-1938 Indian Type II

Designed by: James E. Fraser
Issue dates: 1913-1938
Composition: 0.75 part copper, 0.25 part nickel
Diameter: 21.2 mm
Weight: 77.16 grains (5 grams)
Edge: Plain
Business strike mintage: 1,174,464,771
Proof mintage: 4,439 Matte Proofs; 10,189 Proofs with brilliant finish

The Type II Buffalo nickel is similar to the Type I of 1913 except for the reverse. The Type II features a restyled area at the bottom of the reverse. The "buffalo," previously standing on a raised mound, is now on a line or plane. The inscription FIVE CENTS, earlier on the mound, is now in a recessed portion below the line, thus protecting it from wear. This style was produced from 1913 through the end of the Buffalo motif in 1938.

The type set collector will have no difficulty in obtaining one of the commoner issues of this style, perhaps a piece in the 1930s. Examples are available in all grades from About Good through superb Uncirculated. Most surviving Buffalo nickels show areas of light striking in one part of the design or another, with the high parts of the Indian's head often being indistinct. Indeed, certain issues of the Denver and San Francisco mints in the 1920s are nearly always weakly struck, with 1926-D being particularly egregious in this regard. Sharply struck and minutely detailed business strike Buffalo nickels of *any* date are scarce. Matte Proofs were minted from 1913 through 1916 and closely resemble business strikes except that the Matte Proof issues have brilliant squared-off edges and rims and have a microscopically granular surface, unlike the mint "frost" of most business strikes. Often an expert must be enlisted to tell the difference. In 1936 and 1937 Proofs of the brilliant finish were produced.

NICKEL FIVE-CENT PIECE
1938 to Date, Jefferson

Designed by: Felix O. Schlag
Issue dates: 1938 to date
Composition: 0.75 part copper, 0.25 part nickel
Diameter: 21.2 mm
Weight: 76.16 grains (5 grams)
Edge: Plain
Business strike mintage: 21,158,380,137 through 1985
Proof mintage: 78,735,299 through 1985

In 1938 the nickel was redesigned. Entering a competition with 390 artists, Felix Schlag captured an award of $1,000 for his motif picturing Thomas Jefferson on the obverse and a corner view of Jefferson's home, Monticello, on the reverse. In the final production design, the profile of Monticello was changed to a front view. The finished product depicted a head and shoulders portrait of Jefferson facing left, with IN GOD WE TRUST to the left and LIBERTY and the date to the right. The reverse depicted Monticello at the center, E PLURIBUS UNUM above, and inscriptions of MONTICELLO, FIVE CENTS, and UNITED STATES OF AMERICA below. Certain issues from 1942 through 1945 were made of a different metallic composition and are known as "wartime" nickels and are discussed in the next listing. Apart from these, the type has remained the same from 1938 onward. In 1966 the initials of the designer, FS, were added to the obverse edge beneath the shoulder. However, collectors have not considered this addition to represent a major type.

Jefferson nickels, currently being produced, are readily available in all grades. Business strikes with sharply-struck steps on the Monticello building are scarce for certain issues, but searching for these is in the realm of the Jefferson nickel specialist and need not concern the collector seeking a single specimen for type.

NICKEL FIVE-CENT PIECE
1942-1945 Wartime Jefferson

Designed by: Felix O. Schlag
Issue dates: 1942-1945
Composition: .56 part silver, .09 part manganese
Diameter: 21.2 mm
Weight: 77.16 grains (5 grams)
Edge: plain
Business strike mintage: 869,896,100
Proof mintage: 27,600

The so-called "wartime" alloy represents a World War II measure to eliminate the use of nickel, a strategic material, in coinage. The former composition of 0.75 part copper and 0.25 nickel was changed to 0.56 part copper, 0.35 part silver, and 0.9 part manganese. To differentiate the new alloy and to aid in later redemption and sorting by metallic content of these pieces by the Treasury Department, the wartime pieces were made with a large mintmark above the dome of Monticello. The Philadelphia Mint, which had never used a mintmark earlier, was represented by a P, while Denver and San Francisco were represented by D and S respectively. I believe it was Philadelphia dealer Harry Forman who first called these "wartime" issues. In recent decades they have been popularly collected as a distinct set.

Business strikes are readily available in grades from Very Good to superb Uncirculated. Worn pieces are apt to have a rather scruffy appearance, so the acquisition of an Uncirculated (or Proof) piece is recommended. Uncirculated coins are usually sharply struck. In 1942, 27,600 Proofs were made of the wartime alloy at the Philadelphia Mint, each coin being distinguished by a P above the dome. These pieces are readily available today, although the demand for them by type collectors has caused the price to rise sharply in recent decades.

DIME
1916-1945 Mercury

Designed by: Adolph A. Weinman
Issue dates: 1916-1945
Composition: 0.900 part silver, 0.100 part copper
Diameter: 17.9 mm
Weight: 38.58 grains
Edge: Reeded
Business strike mintage: 2,677,153,880
Proof mintage: 78,648

In 1916, sculptor Adolph A. Weinman produced a new design for the dime. Called the Liberty Head type at the time, the motif features Miss Liberty facing left, wearing a Phrygian cap with wings, LIBERTY encircling her head, and with IN GOD WE TRUST and the date below. The wings on the cap gave rise to the popular term "Mercury dime" for the winged messenger. But, Mercury was a male in mythology and had wings on his *feet*. Nevertheless, the name has stuck, and Mercury dimes are what collectors know them as today. The reverse depicts a fasces or bundle of sticks with a blade at the top, against a branch in the background, and with UNITED STATES OF AMERICA and ONE DIME around the border. E PLURIBUS UNUM appears at the lower right. The design was continued without change through 1945. Coinage was accomplished at the Philadelphia, Denver, and San Francisco mints. Proofs were made at Philadelphia from 1936 through 1942.

Examples of the Mercury dime type are readily available in all grades from About Good through superb Uncirculated. Certain issues are lightly struck and are apt to have weaknesses on the bands tying the sticks in the fasces on the reverse. Those with sharply defined bands, designated as "full split bands," are worth more for many issues.

DIME
1946-1964 Roosevelt, Silver

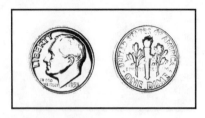

Designed by: John R. Sinnock
Issue dates: 1946-1964 (in silver alloy)
Composition: 0.900 part silver, 0.100 part copper
Diameter: 17.9 mm
Weight: 38.58 grains
Edge: Reeded
Business strike mintage: 6,595,617,673
Proof mintage: 19,837,717

After the death of President Franklin D. Roosevelt in 1945 it was decided to redesign the so-called Mercury dime to reflect the former president's portrait. The dime denomination was selected because Roosevelt had a close association with the March of Dimes charity fundraising over a long period of years. John R. Sinnock, chief engraver at the Philadelphia Mint, produced a portrait showing the head of Roosevelt facing left, with LIBERTY at the left side of the coin, IN GOD WE TRUST below his chin, and the date to the lower right. The reverse depicts a torch with branches to each side, with UNITED STATES OF AMERICA and ONE DIME around the borders. E PLURIBUS UNUM is placed among the branch stems and torch base. In the alloy of 0.900 part silver and 0.100 part copper, the design was produced from 1946 through 1964, after which time the alloy was changed (see next chapter). Production was accomplished at the Philadelphia, Denver, and San Francisco mints. Proofs were made at Philadelphia from 1950 through 1964.

The type collector will have no difficulty obtaining an example in any grade desired from Very Fine to superb Uncirculated. In addition, Proofs survive in large quantities.

QUARTER DOLLAR
1916-1917 Standing Liberty Type I

Designed by: Hermon A. MacNeil
Issue dates; 1916-1917
Compositon: 0.900 part silver, 0.100 part copper
Diameter: 23.4 mm
Weight: 96.45 grains
Edge: Reeded
Business strike mintage: 12,253,200
Proof mintage: None

In 1916 Hermon A. MacNeil, a well-known sculptor, produced a new design for the quarter dollar, replacing the familiar Barber motif which had been employed since 1892. The obverse depicts Miss Liberty standing in a gateway, her right breast exposed, wearing a gown, holding a branch in her right hand and a shield in her left. LIBERTY is in an arc above, while IN GOD WE TRUST is lettered on the wall or parapet to each side of where she stands. The date is on a pedestal beneath her feet. The reverse shows an eagle flying to the right, with UNITED STATES OF AMERICA and E PLURIBUS UNUM above, with QUARTER DOLLAR below. Seven stars are to the left and six to the right. 52,000 were minted in 1916, followed by generous mintage of over 10,000,000 at the three mints in 1917. Complaints arose concerning the partial nudity of Miss Liberty, and because of this the design was soon changed (see the following listing).

While examples of the 1916 date are rare, the type set collector desiring a Standing Liberty quarter of 1917 will have no difficulty in acquiring one from any desired grade from Good through AU. Uncirculated pieces are fairly scarce, while superb Uncirculated coins are very elusive. Unlike their later counterparts, Type I quarters are usually sharply struck at Miss Liberty's head and on the shield. Most Uncirculated pieces possess full details.

QUARTER DOLLAR
1917-1930 Standing Liberty, Type II

Designed by: Hermon A. MacNeil
Issue dates: 1917-1930
Composition: 0.900 part silver, 0.100 part copper
Diameter: 23.4 mm
Weight: 96.45 grains
Edge: Reeded
Business strike mintage: 214,516,400
Proof strike mintage: None

Complaints arose concerning the exposed right breast of Miss Liberty, so partway through 1917 the design was changed. The new Miss Liberty now appears safely and nearly completely encased in a suit of armor or mail, perhaps a classic situation of overcompensation! The date, high on the pedestal below Miss Liberty, was continued in this position, but later, in 1925, this portion of the coin was recessed, to minimize the effects of wear. The reverse was restyled in 1917 and in its new form the eagle is higher and more centered on the coin, with three stars below the eagle and five to each side. The so-called Type II quarter was produced from 1917 through 1930, continuously except for the year 1922. Although Congress earlier mandated that coining design should not be changed more often than each 25 years, by the early 1930s it was decided to discontinue the Standing Liberty motif in favor of a new design (see following listing).

The collector will have no difficulty acquiring specimens of commoner dates of the 1917-1930 era in any desired condition from Good to AU. Uncirculated pieces are readily found, particularly of dates from 1925 through 1930. Uncirculated pieces with sharply struck details at Miss Liberty's head and also on the highest part of the shield are quite elusive, and for some issues (such as 1926-D) are very rare. Such pieces often command a sharp premium over normal Uncirculated coins. No Proofs were minted during this span.

QUARTER DOLLAR
1932-1964 Washington, Silver

Designed by: John Flanagan
Issue dates: 1932-1964
Composition: 0.900 part silver, 0.100 part copper
Diameter: 24.3 mm
Weight: 96.45 grains
Edge: Reeded
Business strike mintage: 3,780,077,001
Proof mintage: 19,911,592

In observance of the 200th anniversary of George Washington's birth, the government decided to redesign the quarter dollar to depict the image of our first president. A lively competition ensued, and picked from this was a proposal of John Flanagan, a New York sculptor. The obverse of the Washington quarter dollar shows the head of Washington, modeled after a bust by Houdon, facing left, with LIBERTY above, IN GOD WE TRUST to the left, and the date below. The reverse shows a modernistic perched eagle, with a wreath below and E PLURIBUS UNUM above. UNITED STATES OF AMERICA and QUARTER DOLLAR inscriptions are at the borders. In silver alloy the type was minted continuously from 1932 to 1964, with the exception of 1933. After 1964, a new alloy was used (see next chapter).

The type set collector can readily obtain a later date in the series for low cost, in any desired condition from well-worn to superb Uncirculated. In addition, Proofs are available of the years 1936 through 1942 and 1950 through 1964.

HALF DOLLAR
1916-1947 Walking Liberty

Designed by: Adolph A. Weinman
Issue dates: 1916-1947
Composition: 0.900 part silver, 0.100 part copper
Diameter: 30.6 mm
Weight: 192.9 grains
Edge: Reeded
Business strike mintage: 485,320,340
Proof mintage: 74,400

In 1916 the design of Adolph A. Weinman was selected for the new half dollar motif to replace the Barber design which had been in use since 1892. Weinman, a sculptor, also produced the Liberty Head or "Mercury" dime introduced the same year. The obverse depicts Miss Liberty walking toward the sun, her right arm outstretched, her left arm carrying a bundle of branches, and with a starry cape behind. LIBERTY is above, while IN GOD WE TRUST is to the lower right, and the date is below. The motif seems to have been inspired by Saint-Gaudens' motif for the illustrious double eagle of 1907. The reverse shows an eagle perched on a rocky crag, from which grows a pine branch, symbol of strength. UNITED STATES OF AMERICA is above, E PLURIBUS UNUM is to the left, and HALF DOLLAR is below. The design has been a favorite with numismatists ever since the time of issue, and many consider it to be one of the most beautiful motifs ever employed on a circulating coin.

Specimens of the Liberty Walking half dollar are readily available for the type collector, with those dated in the 1940s being most easily found. Grades available range from Good through superb Uncirculated, although sharply struck pieces are decidedly scarce. Proofs were minted from 1936 through 1942 and are available in proportion to the original mintages.

HALF DOLLAR
1948-1963 Franklin

Designed by: John R. Sinnock
Issue dates: 1948-1963
Composition: 0.900 part silver, 0.100 part copper
Diameter: 30.6 mm
Weight: 192.9 grains
Edge: Reeded
Business strike mintage: 465,814,455
Proof mintage: 15,886,955

In 1948 John R. Sinnock, chief engraver of the Philadelphia Mint, produced a new design for the half dollar, to replace the Liberty Walking motif which had been in use since 1916. The Franklin half dollar depicts a head and shoulders portrait of Franklin on the obverse, facing right, with LIBERTY above and IN GOD WE TRUST below. The date is to the right. The reverse shows the Liberty Bell with UNITED STATES OF AMERICA above and HALF DOLLAR below. The motto E PLURIBUS UNUM is to the left while a small eagle is to the right. At the time of issue, the design was criticized by many, perhaps because it is rather plain in comparison to the "classic" Liberty Walking style. However, in recent years Franklin half dollars have emerged as popular pieces, and today they are highly desired by numismatists.

The type set collector can easily obtain a business strike in any desired grade from Very Fine to superb Uncirculated, although sharply struck Uncirculated pieces showing full bell lines on the reverse and other minutely detailed areas are elusive for some issues. Proofs were minted from 1950 through 1964 and are available in proportion to their original production quantities.

SILVER DOLLAR
1921-1935 Peace

Designed by: Anthony DeFrancisci
Issue dates: 1921-1935
Composition: 0.900 part silver, 0.100 part copper
Diameter: 38.1 mm
Weight: 412.5 grains
Edge: Reeded
Business strike mintage: 190,577,279
Proof mintage: Fewer than 50 in 1921-1922

The so-called Peace silver dollar, designed by Anthony DeFrancisci, was first produced in December 1921, following a large mintage of Morgan dollars that same year. The Peace dollar depicts on the obverse Miss Liberty, facing left, wearing a diadem of spikes. LIBERTY is above, while IN GOD WE TRUST and the date are below. The reverse shows an eagle perched on a rock, with a laurel branch, and with PEACE inscribed below. UNITED STATES OF AMERICA and E PLURIBUS UNUM are above, while ONE DOLLAR is to be seen just below the center. Rays of an unseen sun emanate from the lower right. Issues of 1921, and a few pieces dated 1922, are in high relief, although collectors have not necessarily differentiated this as a distinct design. It was found that the high relief caused problems in having the pieces strike up properly, so in 1922 the motifs were redone to a shallower format, a style continued through 1935. Mintage of Peace silver dollars was continuous from 1921 through 1928 and again in 1934 and 1935.

Specimens of the common issues from 1921 through 1925 are readily obtainable in various grades from Very Fine through Uncirculated. Sharply struck Uncirculated pieces with full lustre and with a minimum of marks are quite scarce.

Chapter 8

New Issues
COPPER, NICKEL AND SILVER
1951 ONWARD

The new designs instituted from 1951 onward are familiar to everyone. Here, literally, is the coinage of our own time.

In 1959, after a span of 50 years during which the wreath motif was used on the reverse of the Lincoln cent, the reverse was redesigned to illustrate the Lincoln Memorial. A further cent type was created in 1982 when copper plated zinc was employed in place of the earlier bronze alloy. It was feared at the time that the rising price of bulk copper would soon see Lincoln cents worth more in melt-down value than in face value, something which happened several times with silver and gold in American coinage history.

The rising price of silver in 1964 made it obvious that continued production of the metal would result in coins being worth more intrinsicly than the face value stated. There were several alternatives. The silver content could be reduced in the alloy, thus lowering the metallic worth. Or, the alloy could remain the same, but the coins could be made thinner and lighter. Or, a new metallic composition could be used. The latter is what happened, and beginning in 1965 the dime, quarter, and half dollar were all made in clad alloy, although silver continued as part of the alloy to make half dollars through 1970. By the time that the United States in effect dropped silver from the coinage roster in 1965, much of the rest of the world had done the same. The removal of silver from new coins and the withdrawal from circulation of earlier silver coins precipitated a nationwide interest in the bright metal, with the result that before long, quantities of circulated earlier coins were trading at sharp premiums above face value. About 15 years later silver reached a peak, brushing the $50 per ounce mark briefly. Silver made front-page headlines as the Hunt brothers of Texas attempted to amass large quantities. Later, the interest waned, and over the next several years the price

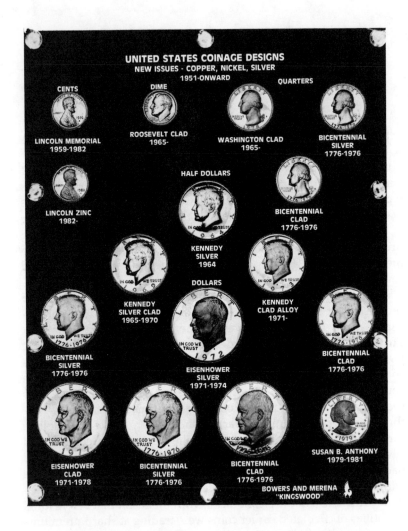

UNITED STATES COINAGE DESIGNS
NEW ISSUES - COPPER, NICKEL, SILVER
1951-ONWARD

CENTS

DIME

QUARTERS

LINCOLN MEMORIAL
1959-1982

ROOSEVELT CLAD
1965-

WASHINGTON CLAD
1965-

BICENTENNIAL
SILVER
1776-1976

HALF DOLLARS

LINCOLN ZINC
1982-

BICENTENNIAL
CLAD
1776-1976

KENNEDY
SILVER
1964

KENNEDY
SILVER CLAD
1965-1970

DOLLARS

KENNEDY
CLAD ALLOY
1971-

BICENTENNIAL
SILVER
1776-1976

EISENHOWER
SILVER
1971-1974

BICENTENNIAL
CLAD
1776-1976

EISENHOWER
CLAD
1971-1978

BICENTENNIAL
SILVER
1776-1976

BICENTENNIAL
CLAD
1776-1976

SUSAN B. ANTHONY
1979-1981

BOWERS AND MERENA
"KINGSWOOD"

Coinage of our own time is the topic of the "Kingswood" display
holder shown above. While no type in this span is a rarity, all have
interesting stories to tell.

164

drifted downward to below $5 per ounce, but still significantly higher than it was when silver coinage ceased in 1965.

In 1964, the last year of general silver coinage, a new half dollar design appeared. Featuring John F. Kennedy, the motif replaced the Franklin design which had been used since 1948. Numismatists welcomed the change, for at the time the Franklin style was viewed by many as being inartistic. The historical memory of Kennedy and his popularity were such that from the outset half dollars bearing his image were intensely hoarded. Eventually, hundreds of millions were squirreled away, thus resulting in the nearly complete disappearance of the denomination from circulation. As new vending machines were made, most were equipped with slots permitting coins no larger than a quarter dollar. By the mid-1980s, half dollars were rarely seen and could be obtained in quantity only by applying for them at banks. For all practical purposes, coins in circulation were reduced to just four values: the cent, nickel, dime, and quarter.

The dollar denomination was produced for circulation again in 1971, following a lapse since 1935. The new Eisenhower dollar was made of clad metal, although some special silver-content versions were struck for collectors. The Eisenhower dollar, minted in various forms from 1971 through 1978, was created primarily in response to gambling casinos in Las Vegas which desired dollar-size coins for the gaming tables. Except for this use, Eisenhower dollars never circulated widely.

In 1979 a new idea reared its head. A study showed that a paper dollar had a useful life of about 18 *months* in circulation, whereas a coin might be useful for 16 *years* or more. The Treasury Department noted that in France and England, for example, paper currency of smaller denominations was successfully supplanted by coins. It was felt that a dollar-size coin would be economical and would save the printing of countless millions of dollar bills. At the same time it was realized that the large diameter of the Eisenhower dollar was cumbersome. Accordingly, a new size was decided upon, a size between the familiar quarter and half dollar. Designs were prepared at the Mint, and Chief Engraver Frank Gasparro created a Liberty Head design somewhat similar to that used on the cent and half cent of 1793. This motif caused wide admiration among collectors. However, Congress was persuaded to honor Susan B. Anthony, a champion of women's rights, and Gasparro was directed to produce an Anthony design. Susan Anthony dollars were struck by the hundreds of millions and placed in circulation in 1979. From the outset, there was a hue and cry against them. Many confused them with the quarter dollar, and numerous tales were told of Anthony dollars being thrown into turnpike toll machines or given in change as quarter dollars. Launched during the wildly inflationary presidency of

Jimmy Carter, the Anthony dollar took the brunt of much public criticism against inflation itself. Although additional Susan Anthony dollars were minted in 1980 and 1981, from an early time the coin was recognized as a failure, a numismatic dodo somewhat similar to the 20-cent piece of a century earlier. Still, the pieces were and are popular with collectors, representing as they do a coin from our own time with an interesting story to tell.

The bicentennial year of 1976 saw new designs for the quarter dollar, half dollar, and dollar, all of which retained their standard Washington, Kennedy, or Eisenhower obverses but had the interesting double date 1776-1976. The reverse of each was distinctive and was selected from a nationwide competition of artists.

There are no rarities among these coins of our own time, and a beautiful set in superb condition can be assembled for moderate cost.

CENT
1959-1982 Memorial Reverse, Bronze

Designed by: Victor D. Brenner (obverse); Frank Gasparro
(reverse)
Issue dates: 1959-1982
Composition: 1959-1962 0.95 part copper, 0.05 part tin and zinc;
1962-1982 0.95 part copper, 0.05 part zinc
Diameter: 19 mm
Weight: 48 grains
Edge: Plain
Business strike mintage: 158,150,469,076*
Proof mintage: 65,103,802

In 1959 the reverse of the Lincoln cent was restyled. The former
wreath motif was discarded in favor of a plan view of the Lincoln
Memorial, a design by Frank Gasparro of the United States Mint.
Above the building the motto E PLURIBUS UNUM appears, while
UNITED STATES OF AMERICA and ONE CENT are around the border. The obverse remains the same as used in earlier years. This style,
made in "bronze" from 1959 to 1962, had a composition of 0.95 part
copper and 0.05 part tin and zinc. In 1962 the alloy was changed
slightly to 0.95 part copper and 0.05 part zinc. Lincoln cents of this
style were made in large quantities, with numerous issues exceeding the billion mark. Although in an era in which the cent piece had
virtually no purchasing power on its own, and in which logic would
suggest that the denomination would be obsolete, the proliferation
of state and local sales taxes made the cent more important than ever
to facilitate making change. Thus, during this span cents were
produced in record quantities, exceeding for the first time the ten
billion mark in 1982.

Examples of the 1959-1982 cent are easily obtainable in any grade
desired.

*1982 zinc cent mintage included in this figure.

CENT
1982 to Date, Copper-Coated Zinc

Designed by: Victor D. Brenner (obverse); Frank Gasparro (reverse)

Issue dates: 1982 to date

Composition: planchet consisting of 0.992 part zinc and 0.008 part copper, with an external plating of pure copper

Diameter: 19 mm

Weight: 38.58 grains

Edge: Plain

Business strike mintage: 38,179,177,147 through 1985

Proof mintage: 9,813,065 through 1985

By 1982 the price of copper had risen to the point at which Treasury officials feared that cents would be hoarded for their metallic content. To forestall this and also to permit production of cents at lower cost, the earlier alloy consisting primarily of copper was replaced with a new format consisting of a core composed of 0.992 part zinc and 0.008 part copper with an external plating of pure copper, resulting in a total metallic content for the issue of 0.976 part zinc and 0.024 part copper. In the year 1982 the earlier as well as the later metallic compositions were employed. The idea proved to be a success, and by 1986 Mint Director Donna Pope stated that cents were in abundant supply and that there was no hint of public hoarding. By that time the run-up in copper prices, characteristic of the activity in nearly all metals markets during the early 1980s, had subsided. As a current coin, the Lincoln cent type from 1982 to date has been produced in large quantities and probably will be produced in large quantities in years to come.

Specimens are readily available in Uncirculated and Proof finishes.

*1982 zinc cent mintage not included.

DIME
1965 to Date, Roosevelt Clad

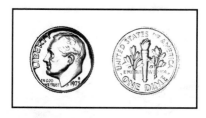

Designed by: John R. Sinnock
Issue dates: 1965 to date
**Composition: Pure copper core to which a copper-nickel (0.75
    part copper, 0.25 part nickel) is bonded**
Diameter: 17.9 mm
Weight: 35.03 grains
Edge: Reeded
Business strike mintage: 24,235,737,852 through 1985
Proof mintage: 58,803,304 through 1985

In 1965, following the discontinuation of silver for nearly all American coinage, the dime was first produced in an innovative format known as "clad" coinage. An outer layer consisting of copper-nickel, composed of 0.75 part copper and 0.25 part nickel, somewhat resembling silver in appearance, was bonded to a core of pure copper. The copper core is visible at the edge. The design of the Roosevelt dime, in use since 1946, remained the same. Only the composition differed. The clad style coinage has been produced continuously since 1965.

Examples of this current format are readily available in Uncirculated and Proof grades.

QUARTER DOLLAR
1965 to Date, Clad

Designed by: John Flanagan
Issue dates: 1965 to date
Composition: Pure copper core to which a copper nickel (0.75
part copper, 0.25 part nickel) is bonded
Diameter: 24.3 mm
Weight: 87.5 grains
Edge: Reeded
Business strike mintage: 17,622,140,990 through 1985
Proof mintage: 51,808,124 through 1985

Following the mintage of the last silver quarter dollars for circulation in 1964, the Mint produced, beginning in 1965, the Washington
design using "clad" planchets. As is the case with the dime, the planchet composition consists of a core of pure copper to which are bonded upper and lower layers of copper-nickel metal, silver in appearance, consisting of 0.75 part copper and 0.25 part nickel. This format
has remained in use to the present day. Production was interrupted
in 1976 by the special bicentennial motif, discussed in the next listing.

Examples of the clad style, currently in use, are readily available
in Uncirculated and Proof finishes.

QUARTER DOLLAR
1776-1976 Bicentennial, Clad

Designed by: John Flanagan (obverse); Jack L. Ahr (reverse)
Issue date: 1976
Composition: Pure copper core to which a copper nickel (0.75 part copper, 0.25 part nickel) is bonded
Diameter: 24.3 mm
Weight: 87.5 grains
Edge: Reeded
Business strike mintage: 1,669,902,855
Proof mintage: 7,059,099

To observe the nation's bicentennial the Treasury Department called for a competition to redesign the reverses of the quarter, half dollar, and dollar. The motif submitted by Jack L. Ahr was the winner for the quarter. At the center of the coin a drummer in colonial garb is shown, with a torch encircled by stars to the upper left, with E PLU-RIBUS UNUM below it. The inscription UNITED STATES OF AMERICA, QUARTER DOLLAR surrounds. The obverse of the coin is a continuation of the design by John Flanagan inaugurated in 1932, except that the bicentennial piece has the unique concept (in American coinage for circulation) of a double date: 1776-1976. Examples were produced in large quantities for circulation at the Philadelphia and Denver mints. At the San Francisco Mint Proofs were made for collectors. Interestingly, production was well underway in 1975, the year *before* the bicentennial, thus creating *pre*strikes.

Uncirculated and Proof pieces are readily available.

QUARTER DOLLAR
1776-1976 Bicentennial, Silver Clad

Designed by: John Flanagan (obverse); Jack L. Ahr (reverse)
Issue date: 1976
Composition: Layers of 0.8 part silver and 0.2 part copper bonded
   to core of 0.209 part silver, 0.791 part copper
Diameter: 24.3 mm
Weight: 88.73 grains
Edge: Reeded
Business strike mintage: 11,000,000
Proof mintage: 4,000,000

The San Francisco Mint produced an additional coinage of bicentennial coins with high silver content. The "clad" format was used, with the outer layers consisting of 0.8 part silver and 0.2 part copper bonded to a core of 0.209 part silver and 0.791 part copper. 11,000,000 were struck with a business or "Uncirculated" finish, while 4,000,000 Proofs were made. Unsold examples of both finishes remained in the Mint inventory for a number of years after they were produced.

Uncirculated and Proof specimens are readily available.

HALF DOLLAR
1964 Kennedy, Silver

Designed by: Gilroy Roberts (obverse); Frank Gasparro (reverse)
Issue date: 1964
Composition: 0.900 part silver, 0.100 part copper
Diameter: 30.6 mm
Weight: 192.9 grains
Edge: Reeded
Business strike mintage: 429,509,450
Proof mintage: 3,950,962

Following the assassination of President John Fitzgerald Kennedy in November 1963, plans were made to memorialize the popular president on circulating half dollars. Gilroy Roberts, chief engraver of the Mint, designed the obverse. The reverse was the work of Frank Gasparro. The obverse design depicts the head of Kennedy facing left, with LIBERTY above and to the sides and the date below. IN GOD WE TRUST is in a straight line above the date. The reverse is an adaptation of the Great Seal of the United States and is reminiscent of the Heraldic Eagle style used on gold and silver coinage of the 1800 era. The Kennedy half dollar captured the public's imagination, and pieces sold at a premium from the very moment of release. Soon the premiums subsided, but despite mintages of hundreds of millions of coins, few were used in the channels of commerce. Subsequently, the half dollar became an obsolete denomination so far as everyday use is concerned. Still, large quantities were produced, although mintage figures trended downward over a period of time. After 1964, the silver content was modified, thus isolating the 1964 year as the only Kennedy half dollar composed of nine parts silver and one part copper.

Specimens today are readily available in Uncirculated and Proof finishes.

HALF DOLLAR
1965-1970 Kennedy, Silver Clad

Designed by: Gilroy Roberts (obverse), Frank Gasparro (reverse)
Issue dates: 1965-1970
Composition: Outer layers of 0.8 part silver and 0.2 part copper bonded to core of 0.209 part silver, 0.791 part copper.
Diameter: 30.6 mm
Weight: 177.46 grains
Edge: Reeded
Business strike mintage: 848,895,006
Proof mintage: 8,608,947

In 1965, and continuing through 1970, the composition of the half dollar was modified to diminish its silver content. Unlike the dime and quarter denominations, the half dollar retained some silver, however. The new style was made by sandwiching outer layers consisting of eight parts silver and two parts copper to a core of 0.209 part silver and 0.791 part copper, giving the coin a "silver" appearance. Whereas the 1964 Kennedy half dollar contained a net of 0.3617 ounce of pure silver, the 1965-1970 clad coinage saw a reduced content of 0.1479 ounce, making it unprofitable at the time to melt them down for their bullion value. Later, with the run-up in metal prices in the 1980 period, the 1965-1970 silver-clad pieces became worth more in meltdown value than face value, thus causing the destruction of many.

Examples are readily available in Uncirculated and Proof finishes.

HALF DOLLAR
1971 to Date, Kennedy, Clad

Designed by: Gilroy Roberts (obverse), Frank Gasparro (reverse)
Issue dates: 1971 to date
Composition: Outer layers of .75 part copper and .25 part
  nickel bonded to inner core of pure copper.
Diameter: 30.6 mm
Weight: 175 grains
Edge: Reeded
Business strike mintage: 1,684,775,933 through 1985
Proof mintage: 43,199,177 through 1985

Beginning in 1971, and continuing through the present time, the composition of the half dollar was modified to conform to that of the dime and quarter. The current style consists of a core of pure copper with outer layers of copper-nickel, with a silvery appearance, consisting of 0.75 part copper and 0.25 part nickel. The Kennedy obverse and Heraldic Eagle reverse, in use since 1964, were continued. Business strikes were produced by the Philadelphia and Denver mints, while San Francisco made Proofs for collectors. The standard style was interrupted in 1976 by the bicentennial motif (see following listing). When coinage resumed in 1977, after the bicentennial observance, mintages in the Kennedy series for the first time were fewer than 100 million per year.

Examples are easily obtainable in Uncirculated and Proof finishes.

HALF DOLLAR
1776-1976 Bicentennial, Clad

Designed by: Gilroy Roberts (obverse); Seth G. Huntington (reverse)

Issue date: 1976

Composition: Outer layers of 0.800 silver, 0.200 copper bonded to inner core of 0.210 silver, 0.790 copper; copper-nickel clad: weight 11.34 grams; composition: outer layers of copper-nickel (0.750 copper, 0.250 nickel) bonded to inner core of pure copper.

Diameter: 30.6 mm.

Weight: 175 grains

Edge: Reeded

Business strike mintage: 521,873,248

Proof mintage: 7,059,099

In 1976 a special reverse was employed for the 1776-1976 dated Kennedy half dollar. The obverse remained the same as used earlier, except for the date, while the reverse displayed a new design by Seth G. Huntington, a Minnesota artist who entered the national competition for bicentennial motifs. Shown at the center of the coin is a representation of Independence Hall in Philadelphia, somewhat similar to that used earlier (in 1926) on the reverse of the sesquicentennial gold quarter eagle. To the left of the building is the inscription 200 YEARS OF FREEDOM, while to the right is the motto E PLURIBUS UNUM, with INDEPENDENCE HALL and an arc of stars below. The inscription UNITED STATES OF AMERICA, HALF DOLLAR surrounds. Over 500,000,000 business strikes were produced at the Philadelphia and Denver mints, while the San Francisco facility turned out 7,059,099 Proofs.

Specimens are readily available in Uncirculated and Proof formats.

HALF DOLLAR
1776-1976 Bicentennial, Silver, Clad

Designed by: Gilroy Roberts (obverse); Seth G. Huntington (reverse)
Issue date: 1976
Composition: Layers of 0.8 part silver and 0.2 part copper bonded to core of 0.209 part silver, 0.791 part copper
Diameter: 30.6 mm
Weight: 177.47 grains
Edge: Reeded
Business strike mintage: 11,000,000
Proof mintage: 4,000,000

Following the procedure employed for the quarter and dollar denominations, 1776-1976 Kennedy bicentennial half dollars, with Seth G. Huntington's Independence Hall reverse, were produced for collectors, employing a silver clad format consisting of a core of 0.209 part silver and 0.791 part copper with outer layers consisting of 0.8 part silver and 0.2 part copper, giving the pieces a silver appearance. 11,000,000 business strikes or "Uncirculated" pieces and 4,000,000 Proofs were struck, all at the San Francisco Mint. The production was sufficiently large that unsold quantities remained on hand for a number of years afterward.

Specimens today are readily available in Uncirculated and Proof finishes.

DOLLAR
1971-1978 Eisenhower, Clad

Designed by: Frank Gasparro
Issue dates: 1971-1978
Composition: Core of pure copper clad with 0.75 part copper and
   0.25 nickel, copper-nickel alloy.
Diameter: 38.1 mm
Weight: 350 grains
Edge: Reeded
Business strike mintage: 466,001,887
Proof mintage: 11,751,840

Primarily in response to a demand from Nevada gambling casinos, which desired dollar-size coins for use at the gaming tables in an era in which earlier silver dollars had disappeared from circulation, the Mint introduced a new metallic dollar in 1971. Circulating issues were made of copper-nickel clad material. The obverse and reverse designs, the work of Chief Engraver Frank Gasparro, were innovative. The obverse features the head of President Dwight Eisenhower facing left, with LIBERTY above and IN GOD WE TRUST and the date below, while the reverse is symbolic of the landing of Americans on the moon and was adopted from the Apollo 11 insignia. Shown is an eagle holding an olive branch, landing on the moon, with the earth and the inscription E PLURIBUS UNUM above. The inscription UNITED STATES OF AMERICA, ONE DOLLAR appears at the border. Except for use at the gaming tables in Nevada, few Eisenhower dollars were ever employed in general circulation. The design was interrupted in 1976 by the bicentennial motif (see second following listing).

Examples are available in Uncirculated and Proof finishes, although superb Uncirculated pieces are fairly scarce.

DOLLAR
1971-1974 Eisenhower, Silver, Clad

Designed by: Frank Gasparro
Issue dates: 1971-1974
Composition: Core of 0.209 part silver and 0.791 part copper with
outer layers of 0.8 part silver and 0.2 part copper
Diameter: 38.1
Weight: 379.48 grains
Edge: Reeded
Business strike mintage: 12,844,726
Proof mintage: 8,397,090

To provide an issue for coin collectors, Eisenhower dollars of the 1971-1974 years were struck in a silver clad composition, with the production of these special pieces being accomplished at the San Francisco Mint. Apart from metallic content, the design with President Eisenhower's head on the obverse and an eagle landing on the moon on the reverse is the same as the preceding. The San Francisco Mint produced business strike or "Uncirculated" pieces as well as Proof examples.

Specimens are readily available with Uncirculated and Proof finishes.

DOLLAR
1776-1976 Bicentennial, Clad

Designed by: Frank Gasparro (obverse); Dennis R. Williams
   (reverse)
Issue date: 1976
Composition: Core of pure copper clad with 0.75 part copper and
   0.25 part nickel, copper-nickel alloy
Diameter: 38.1
Weight: 350 grains
Edge: Reeded
Business strike mintage: 220,565,274
Proof mintage: 6,995,180

For the bicentennial observation a new reverse was mated to Frank
Gasparro's Eisenhower obverse. The work of Dennis R. Williams,
who entered a nationwide competition for bicentennial designs, the
reverse depicts the Liberty Bell, similar to that found on the 1948-1963
Franklin half dollar, superimposed on the moon. The motto E PLUR-
IBUS UNUM appears to the lower right. The inscription UNITED
STATES OF AMERICA, ONE DOLLAR surrounds. Examples in
copper-nickel clad metal were produced for circulation at the
Philadelphia and Denver mints. Most saw service in Nevada, but
many were acquired as bicentennial souvenirs by the population at
large. Proofs for collectors were struck at San Francisco.

Examples are readily available in Uncirculated and Proof formats.

DOLLAR
1776-1976 Bicentennial, Silver, Clad

Designed by: Frank Gasparro (obverse); Dennis R. Williams
   (reverse)
Issue date: 1976
Composition: Layers of 0.8 part silver and 0.2 part copper bond-
   ed to core of 0.209 part silver, 0.791 part copper
Diameter: 38.1
Weight: 379.48 grains
Edge: Reeded
Business strike mintage: 11,000,000
Proof mintage: 4,000,000

Examples of the Eisenhower bicentennial dollar with the Liberty
Bell and moon reverse, struck on silver clad planchets, were produced
at San Francisco for collectors. 11,000,000 "Uncirculated" pieces were
made and 4,000,000 Proofs were struck. Sales were not up to expectations, and unsold quantities of both formats remained on hand for
a number of years after the issue date.

Examples are readily available in Uncirculated and Proof finishes.

DOLLAR
1979-1981 Susan B. Anthony

Designed by: Frank Gasparro
Issue dates: 1979-1981
Composition: Core of pure copper; outer layers of 0.75 part copper and 0.25 part nickel
Diameter: 26.5 mm
Weight: 125 grains
Edge: Reeded
Business strike mintage: 857,216,452
Proof mintage: 11,295,064

By 1979, half dollars were rarely seen in circulation. The proliferation of vending machines, arcade machines, and other coin-operated devices, most of which dispensed goods or services worth more than a quarter dollar (the highest denomination coin in general circulation at the time) prompted a call for a convenient coin of high value, while a Treasury-sponsored study showed that a metallic dollar had a useful life in circulation of 16 years or more, as compared to only 18 months for a paper dollar. Thus, the new small-diameter dollar was conceived. Frank Gasparro produced the designs. The obverse depicts Susan Anthony facing to the right, with stars to the left and right and with IN GOD WE TRUST near the right border. LIBERTY is above, and the date is below. The reverse is an adaptation of the motif first used on the 1971 Eisenhower dollar and consists of an eagle landing on the moon, with the earth and E PLURIBUS UNUM above, and the inscription UNITED STATES OF AMERICA, ONE DOLLAR surrounding. From the outset, the public confused the small-diameter dollars with the quarter dollars in circulation. As noted in the introduction to this chapter, resentment was high, and the Anthony dollar was unpopular. Collectors, however, were attracted to the design, and today the various issues are quite collectible.

Specimens are readily available in Uncirculated and Proof finishes.

Chapter 9

New Issues
GOLD
1795-1833

The American gold coin designs which made their initial appearance during the 1795-1833 era are among the rarest of the rare in United States coinage. There is no such thing as a "common" issue among the different varieties, and some are exceedingly rare.

The Act of April 2, 1792 established the Philadelphia Mint and provided for various denominations, including gold coins, the largest of which was to be an eagle weighing 270 grains. Although copper coinage commenced in 1793, gold coins were not minted until two years later, for the chief coiner and assayer each were required to post personal surety bonds in the amount of $10,000 before coinage of precious metals could commence. Later, the bond requirements were reduced and were fulfilled. The first delivery of gold coins occurred on July 31, 1795, when 744 half eagles were transferred, followed by amounts through September totaling 8,707 pieces for the year. The first delivery of eagles, or $10 pieces, took place on September 22, 1795, and consisted of 1,097 pieces. Edgar H. Adams, a student of the denomination, noted that George Washington desired to have gold coins struck before his term of office expired, and this wish was granted in 1795 when Director of the Mint Henry DeSaussure delivered 100 eagles to the President.

In 1792, Congress established the relative value of silver to gold at 17 to 1. This relationship proved to be inaccurate, since in the marketplace for bullion the value more closely approximated 16 to 1, with the result that early gold coins were melted down and sold for more than face value in terms of silver. After 1803, when France officially adopted a ratio of 15½ to 1, vast quantities of gold coins were exported or went to the melting pot.

Gold bullion values and the market value ratio of gold to silver fluctuated during the early years, and each time gold increased in value, large quantities of United States coins were melted. Finally, the Act of June 18, 1834 reduced the weight of gold coins, with the

A $10 gold piece, or eagle, of the first year of issue, 1795. This general obverse style was also used on quarter eagles and half eagles of the time, while the Small Eagle reverse was used only on eagles and half eagles only.

This half eagle, or $5 piece, of 1804 illustrates the Heraldic Eagle reverse, a popular motif used on silver and gold coins of the era. It is one of several adaptations of the Great Seal of the United States used in coinage designs over the years.

The scarce 1820 $5 gold piece, or half eagle, shown above is a member of the elusive Capped Head to Left motif minted from 1813 through 1834. All half eagles of this span are scarce, and a number of them are great rarities.

beneficial effect that later pieces could not be melted for profit, and from that point onward gold coins circulated in the channels of commerce. By that time, all earlier gold coins, commonly called *old tenor* coins in various bullion manuals, were worth more than face value. As coin collectors were virtually non-existent, countless thousands of pieces which would have been numismatically desired later, were destroyed. No better evidence of this practice can be found than by studying the mintage records of $5 gold coins of the 1820s and comparing them to the quantities known today. The extreme example is provided by the 1822 half eagle of which 17,796 were struck, but of which just three solitary examples are known to survive today.

As noted, half eagles and eagles made their initial appearance in 1795. The following year, 1796, saw the debut of the $2½ denomination, or quarter eagle. These three denominations constituted the spectrum of American gold coinage during the 1795-1834 years in question. Later, such denominations as the gold dollar (1849), $3 (1854), $4 (patterns in 1879 and 1880), and $20 (1850) would be introduced.

The formation of a complete type set of early gold coins is a fascinating challenge and is necessarily limited to those with a generous budget. As observed earlier, there are no common pieces in the series, and several types are very rare. The 1796 quarter eagle without obverse stars and the 1808 of the same denomination are particularly significant as representatives of the only years that their respective designs were produced.

QUARTER EAGLE
1796 No Obverse Stars

Designed by: Robert Scot
Issue date: 1796
Composition: 0.9167 part gold, 0.0833 part copper
Diameter: 20 mm
Weight: 67.5 grains
Edge: Reeded
Business strike mintage: 963 (estimated)
Proof mintage: None

The first design in the quarter eagle series is distinguished from the later motif by having no stars on the obverse. Designated as the Capped Bust to Right style, the first quarter eagle of 1796, believed to have been minted to the extent of 963 pieces, features the head and shoulder portrait of Miss Liberty facing right, wearing a cloth cap, with LIBERTY above and the date below. There are no stars in the field. The reverse is of the Heraldic Eagle design similar to that used on gold and silver denominations of the 1800 era. Adapted from the Great Seal of the United States, the center motif depicts an eagle with a shield on its breast, holding an olive branch and arrows in its talons, and in its beak a ribbon inscribed E PLURIBUS UNUM. A galaxy of stars is above, with a group of clouds in an arc extending from one wing to the other. The inscription UNITED STATES OF AMERICA surrounds. There is no mark indicating the denomination.

Of the 963 pieces believed to have been minted, it has been estimated by David Akers, a student of the subject, that perhaps as many as 30 to 40 survive today, although other estimates have been in the range of 15 to 20 pieces. Most of these are in grades from Very Fine to Extremely Fine, although a few higher condition examples exist.

QUARTER EAGLE
1796-1807 Capped Bust, Stars

Designed by: Robert Scot
Issue dates: 1796-1807
Composition: 0.9167 part gold, 0.0833 part copper
Diameter: 20 mm
Weight: 67.5 grains
Edge: Reeded
Business strike mintage: 18,524
Proof mintage: None

Following a brief emission of 1796 quarter eagles without obverse stars, the design was modified to add stars to the left and right of the head. The number of stars and their placement vary from issue to issue, but these have not been collected as separate types, perhaps due to the general rarity of quarter eagles in this span. 1796 quarter eagles with stars have eight stars to the left and eight to the right, for a total of 16, while quarter eagles of the years 1797 through 1807 have 13 stars arranged in various ways. 1797 quarter eagles have seven stars to the left and six to the right, while 1798 quarter eagles have six to the left and seven to the right. 1802/1 quarter eagles have eight left and five right. The year 1806 comes in two varieties, eight left and five right as well as seven left and six right. All quarter eagles within this span are rare. Apart from the addition of stars to the obverse, the motifs are the same as on the previous issue.

While a few Uncirculated examples are known of scattered dates, most quarter eagles known within this date span grade from Very Fine to Extremely Fine, with Very Fine being the norm. In keeping with other gold coins, mint-caused planchet adjustment marks are often seen as are areas of light striking.

QUARTER EAGLE
1808 Capped Bust to Left

Designed by: John Reich
Issue date: 1808
Composition: 0.9167 part gold, 0.0833 part copper
Diameter: 20 mm
Weight: 67.5 grains
Edge: Reeded
Business strike mintage: 2,710
Proof mintage: None

In 1808 John Reich redesigned the quarter eagle. The diameter remained the same as earlier, but the obverse and reverse motifs were changed. Miss Liberty now faces left, wearing a loose cloth cap secured by a band inscribed LIBERTY. Seven stars are to the left and six are to the right, and the date 1808 appears below. The reverse depicts an eagle perched on an olive branch and holding three arrows. The motto E PLURIBUS UNUM is on a band or ribbon above. The inscription UNITED STATES OF AMERICA and 2½ D is around the border. The denomination is stated for the first time on a quarter eagle. The mintage figure of 2,710 on its own would suggest a rarity, but the demand for the coin as the only year of its design type has projected it into the forefront of popular rarities among American gold coins. It is believed that perhaps three or four dozen exist, nearly all of which are in the grades of Very Fine or Extremely Fine, although at least two Uncirculated coins can be accounted for.

QUARTER EAGLE
1821-1834 Capped Head to Left

Designed by: John Reich
Issue dates: 1821-1834
Composition: 0.9167 part gold, 0.0833 part copper
Diameter: 18.5 mm (1821-1827), 18.2 mm (1829-1834)
Weight: 67.5 grains
Edge: Reeded
Business strike mintage: 42,065
Proof mintage: Fewer than 150

No quarter eagles were coined from 1809 through 1820 inclusive. In 1821 the denomination was again produced. The design is similar to that used in 1808, except that the diameter is reduced to 18.5 mm (subsequently further reduced to 18.2 mm in 1829) and the portrait of Miss Liberty appears smaller and is circled by stars. This general style was continued in use through 1834. Mintages in all instances were low, with the production of one variety, the 1826, estimated at just 760 pieces.

All quarter eagles of the 1821-1834 years are rare today. Most examples seen are in grades from Very Fine through AU, although scattered Uncirculated pieces have appeared at auction, as have a few Proofs. It is not unusual for an Uncirculated piece to have a prooflike surface.

HALF EAGLE
1795-1798 Small Eagle Reverse

Designed by: Robert Scot
Issue dates: 1795-1798
Composition: 0.9167 part gold, 0.0833 part copper
Diameter: 25 mm
Weight: 135 grains
Edge: Reeded
Business strike mintage: 18,512
Proof mintage: None

Believed to have been designed by Robert Scot, the first half eagle, representing the first United States gold coin actually put in circulation, is of the design designated by collectors today as the Capped Bust to Right obverse with Small Eagle reverse. The obverse depicts Miss Liberty, wearing a cloth cap, facing right, with LIBERTY to the right above and the date below. The star count arrangement is typically 10 to the left and five to the right, but one variety of 1797 has 16 stars arranged 11 to the left and five to the right. The reverse, believed to have been copied from an ancient cameo, shows an eagle perched on a palm branch holding a wreath aloft in its beak. The inscription UNITED STATES OF AMERICA surrounds. There is no mark or indication of value on the piece. At the time, gold coins were valued in the channels of commerce by their weight and metallic content. Examples were produced from 1795 through 1798, with the last year being a major rarity in the series—a coin of which fewer than a dozen are known to exist.

Several hundred examples survive of various 1795-1798 half eagles with the Small Eagle reverse. Most of these bear the date of the first year of issue, 1795. Most surviving specimens are in grades from Very Fine through AU, but over the years a number have been designated as Uncirculated. Among 1795 half eagles, AU and Uncirculated coins often possess prooflike surfaces.

HALF EAGLE
1795-1807 Heraldic Eagle Reverse

Designed by: Robert Scot
Issue dates: 1795-1807
Composition: 0.9167 part gold, 0.0833 part copper
Diameter: 25 mm
Weight: 135 grains
Edge: Reeded
Business strike mintage: 316,867
Proof mintage: None

In *1798* the reverse of the half eagle was restyled to incorporate the Heraldic Eagle motif. However, at the time it was the Mint's practice to keep earlier-dated dies on hand until they were no longer fit for service. It is believed that in 1798 the Mint combined the new reverse with obverse dies dated 1795 and 1797, thus producing earlier-dated pieces. The motif was continued in service through 1807. The obverse design features Miss Liberty facing right, similar to the preceding issue. The star arrangements vary. The reverse is the Heraldic Eagle motif adopted from the Great Seal of the United States and is similar to that found on silver and other gold coins of the 1800 era. An eagle at the center, with a shield on its breast, holds arrows and an olive branch in its talons and a ribbon inscribed E PLURIBUS UNUM in its beak. Above is a galaxy of stars and an arc of clouds. The inscriptions UNITED STATES OF AMERICA surrounds. There is no mark or indication of value.

Although there are some rarities in the 1795-1807 span of this type, enough examples survive of most issues from 1798 through 1807 that the numismatist will have no difficulty acquiring a representative "type" specimen in Very Fine to AU preservation. Uncirculated coins come on the market occasionally and typically have frosty (rather than prooflike) surfaces.

HALF EAGLE
1807-1812 Capped Draped Bust to Left

Designed by: John Reich
Issue dates: 1807-1812
Composition: 0.9167 part gold, 0.0833 part copper
Diameter: 25 mm
Weight: 135 grains
Edge: Reeded
Business strike mintage: 399,013
Proof mintage: None

In 1807 John Reich redesigned the half eagle. The new style is the forerunner of that adopted a year later for the quarter eagle. The obverse depicts Miss Liberty facing left, wearing a cloth cap inscribed LIBERTY, with seven stars to the left and six to the right. The reverse shows an eagle perched on a palm branch, holding three arrows, with the motto E PLURIBUS UNUM on a ribbon or band above. The legend UNITED STATES OF AMERICA, 5 D. surrounds. This style was produced from 1807 through 1812.

Although there are some scarce die varieties within the 1807-1812 span, there are no rare dates, and the type set collector can choose from virtually any date desired. Specimens are available in all grades, with Very Fine to AU coins appearing on the market with some frequency, (relatively speaking, of course). As stated in the introduction to this chapter, *all* early American gold coins are rare in comparison to later issues. Uncirculated coins are offered from time to time, especially when great collections are dispersed, and typically have frosty rather than prooflike surfaces.

HALF EAGLE
1813-1834 Capped Head to Left

Designed by: John Reich
Issue dates: 1813-1834
Composition: 0.9167 part gold, 0.0833 part copper
Diameter: 25 mm (1813-1829), 22.5 mm (1829-1834)
Weight: 135 grains
Edge: Reeded
Business strike mintage: 1,385,612
Proof mintage: Fewer than 150

In 1813 the John Reich design was modified to a portrait featuring the head and part of the neck of Miss Liberty, facing left, an abbreviated version of the earlier style. In the new version, the stars completely surround the head, and the date is below. The reverse motif remains the same. From 1813 to 1829 half eagles were minted with a diameter of 25 mm. In 1829 the diameter was reduced to 22.5 mm and certain other modifications occurred, under the direction of William Kneass. Technically speaking, the 1829-1834 reduced diameter format can be considered a separate type, but as half eagles of this era are exceedingly rare, most numismatists have been content to consider the span 1813-1834 as a single design. The determination of what is a design type and what isn't is a matter of personal preference. There are many variables, such as the star count and position differences noted, for example, among half eagles of the 1795-1807 Heraldic Eagle reverse style.

Although mintages were fairly generous for many half eagles from 1813 through 1834, nearly all of the issues in this span are great rarities today. The type set collector will have the best luck and the best use of his money if an issue such as 1813, 1814/3, 1818, or 1820 is selected, none of which will be inexpensive, but other issues are apt to be much more costly. The half eagle of the 1813-1834 design type is one of the highlights of a type set of early American gold coins.

EAGLE
1795-1797 Small Eagle Reverse

Designed by: Robert Scot
Issue dates: 1795-1797
Composition: 0.9167 part gold, 0.0833 part copper
Diameter: 33 mm
Weight: 270 grains
Edge: Reeded
Business strike mintage: 13,344
Proof mintage: None

Eagles or $10 pieces made their first appearance in circulation toward the end of 1795. The design of the first issue is similar to that of the contemporary half eagle. On the obverse Miss Liberty is shown wearing a cloth cap, facing right, with stars to the left and right. The reverse, copied from the design of an ancient cameo, depicts an eagle perched on a palm branch holding a wreath aloft in its beak. The inscription UNITED STATES OF AMERICA surrounds. There is no indication of denomination or value on this or the subsequent eagle type.

With a total mintage of fewer than 15,000 pieces, eagles of this design type are rare today. However, with some searching, attractive Very Fine to AU coins can be located. At infrequent intervals Uncirculated pieces appear, usually when great collections are dispersed. Such coins are apt to have prooflike surfaces, a situation especially true of the first year of issue, 1795.

EAGLE
1797-1804 Heraldic Eagle Reverse

Designed by: Robert Scot
Issue dates: 1797-1804
Composition: 0.9167 part gold, 0.0833 part copper
Diameter: 33 mm
Weight: 270 grains
Edge: Reeded
Business strike mintage: 119,248
Proof mintage: None

Beginning with coins dated 1797, the Heraldic Eagle reverse was mated to the obverse style used earlier. In keeping with silver and other gold denominations of the 1800 period, the reverse depicts an eagle with a shield on its breast, holding in its talons a bundle of arrows and an olive branch and in its beak a ribbon inscribed E PLURIBUS UNUM. A galaxy of stars and an arc of clouds is above. The inscription UNITED STATES OF AMERICA surrounds. There is no mark of denomination or value. The obverse remains the same as the preceding, except that the star configuration varies on certain issues. For example, the 1798/7, an overdate, exists with nine stars left and four right and also with seven stars left and six right. No eagles were struck after 1804, as it was felt that because of rising bullion prices the pieces would be melted or exported as soon as they were produced.

The type set collector will find that issues of 1799, 1800, 1801, or 1803 will be the most likely candidates. Examples are typically found in Very Fine to AU condition. Uncirculated pieces are rare. Such coins have frosty surfaces.

Chapter 10

New Issues
GOLD
1834-1900

The span from 1834 through 1900 saw a proliferation of United States gold coin denominations and types. To the previous quarter eagle, half eagle and eagle denominations three new values were added: the gold dollar, $3 gold, and double eagle. A pattern denomination, the $4 gold "stella," was made in 1879 and 1880 but was never produced for circulation (and hence is not studied in the following pages). Some type set collectors opt to include an example of the $4 pattern in their collections, however.

By 1834, the bullion content of American gold coins minted to the earlier standards had risen to the point at which newly-minted pieces could be melted down for a profit above their face value. For this reason, gold coins did not circulate readily. Rather, they were bought by bullion dealers and others who made a profit in their melting. To remedy the situation, Congress passed the Act of June 28, 1834, which reduced the authorized weight of existing denominations. From that point forward, gold coins circulated readily.

Following the January 1848 discovery of gold in quantity on the American River in California, the seeds were sown for the great California Gold Rush, which saw a vast migration westward during the 1849-1850 years. Recovered from the earth and streams were untold quantities of gold, so much that gold became "common" in relation to silver, thus causing a problem with silver coinage. By 1853, the authorized weights of silver coins were reduced to prevent their melting for profit.

Faced with the necessity of converting vast amounts of gold bullion into coins, the Treasury Department devised a new denomination, the $20 gold double eagle, which was produced in pattern form in 1849 and for circulation beginning in 1850. It was much more economical to strike one single $20 piece than two $10 pieces or four $5 pieces to coin the same amount of bullion. Double eagles soon became the "workhorse" coin in the banking system, and large quan-

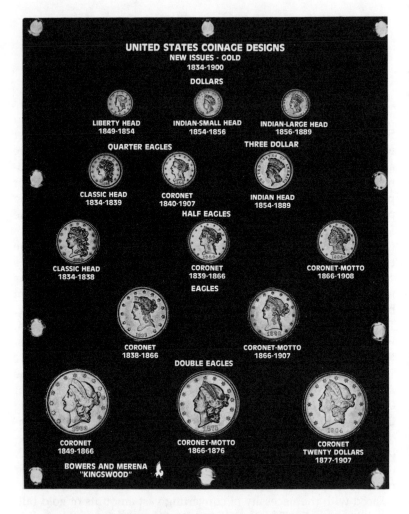

UNITED STATES COINAGE DESIGNS
NEW ISSUES - GOLD
1834-1900

DOLLARS

LIBERTY HEAD
1849-1854

INDIAN-SMALL HEAD
1854-1856

INDIAN-LARGE HEAD
1856-1889

QUARTER EAGLES

THREE DOLLAR

CLASSIC HEAD
1834-1839

CORONET
1840-1907

INDIAN HEAD
1854-1889

HALF EAGLES

CLASSIC HEAD
1834-1838

CORONET
1839-1866

CORONET-MOTTO
1866-1908

EAGLES

CORONET
1838-1866

CORONET-MOTTO
1866-1907

DOUBLE EAGLES

CORONET
1849-1866

CORONET-MOTTO
1866-1876

CORONET
TWENTY DOLLARS
1877-1907

BOWERS AND MERENA
"KINGSWOOD"

The years from 1834 through 1900 saw the emergence of over a dozen new motifs and three new denominations in the American gold coin series. Several of the issues shown here are scarce, particularly the gold dollar style of 1854-1856 and the $3 denomination minted from 1854 through 1889.

The $3 denomination made its appearance in 1854, and was continued through 1889. The obverse is of the Indian Princess style and is similar to that used in gold dollars of the 1856-1889 span. Coins of this denomination were never popular with the public, and production quantities, except for just a few dates, were quite low.

tities were used in bank-to-bank transactions and, in particular, in settlements of overseas transactions in an era in which paper money was viewed with distrust. The practice of exporting large numbers of double eagles continued well into the 20th century. In 1933, when President Franklin Roosevelt called American gold coins in, foreign banking and commercial interests held on to theirs as tightly as ever. This had a beneficial effect for numismatists later when collecting gold coins became popular. For many years, European and South American banks were a major source for such gold coins.

Although pattern gold dollars had been made as early as 1836, it was not until 1849 that the denomination was produced for circulation. The gold dollar proved to be fairly popular, especially in the early days, and was continued in use through 1889. Three different design types were made.

In 1854 still another denomination, the $3 gold piece, made its debut. The $3 had its inception with the bill passed by Congress on February 21, 1853, the main purpose of which was to reduce the authorized weight of all silver pieces except the dollar. The reason for including a $3 piece as part of the legislation has never been satisfactorily explained. Numismatists have theorized that it may have been done as a convenience to buy 3-cent postage stamps in sheets of 100, or to purchase silver three-cent pieces (first issued in 1851) in the same quantity. Considering the closeness in value to the popular $2.50 denomination, the $3 piece seems illogical. But, logic has never prevented Congress from various coinage actions, as numismatic scholars know well! James B. Longacre, chief engraver at the Mint, designed a motif which could not be easily confused with the portrait of Miss Liberty wearing a coronet, which was in use on the contemporary $2.50 and $5 denominations. The result was a distinctive design featuring on the obverse an Indian princess with a feathered headdress and on the reverse a wreath consisting of corn, cotton, wheat, and tobacco. The same obverse and reverse style was to be incorporated on the gold dollar when the design for that denomination was revised in 1854. In 1856 the same wreath was adapted for use on the Flying Eagle cent. The $3 piece was star-crossed, however, and despite early expectations, the denomination was never popular with the public. Finally it was discontinued in 1889, following insignificant mintages in the later years.

In 1834 two existing denominations, the quarter eagle and half eagle, were restyled by William Kneass, thus creating the so-called Classic Head motif, which remained in use through 1838 (for the half eagle) and 1839 (for the quarter eagle).

A new design, variously called the Coronet type, the Liberty Head style, or the Braided Hair design made its appearance on the quarter eagle in 1840, the half eagle in 1839, and the eagle in 1838. This

This 1852 $10 piece, or eagle, is of the Coronet or Liberty Head style and represents the general obverse motif produced from 1838 through 1907 (during which time there were two varieties of reverse styles made).

motif was continued until the early 20th century. Modifications were made to the half eagle, eagle, and double eagle by adding IN GOD WE TRUST beginning in 1866, the same year that the motto was added to several silver denominations.

As a study of individual mintage figures published in *A Guide Book of United States Coins* and elsewhere will reveal, gold coin production figures varied widely during the span under consideration. In general, gold dollars of the 1860-1889 years were made in small quantities as were $3 pieces of the same span. Among quarter eagles of the Coronet type there are many high-mintage issues interspersed with low mintages, with a trend toward increasing production as the Coronet motif entered its final years.

Half eagles of the Coronet type follow a similar trend. The Coronet half eagle is unique in American coinage history inasmuch as this value was struck at all seven of the mints in operation during the 19th and early 20th centuries: Philadelphia, Charlotte, Dahlonega, New Orleans, San Francisco, Carson City, and Denver.

Eagle mintages of the Coronet type follow a similar pattern and increase in quantity toward the end of the design, although a number of earlier varieties have generous mintages as well. Interspersed are numerous rarities. Double eagles were produced in vast quantities from 1850 onward, with the first year of production, 1850, registering the incredible total of over a million pieces, followed by over two million in each of the next two years, the result of converting California bullion. As noted, these were "workhorse" coins and were extensively used in bank-to-bank transactions and overseas financial settlements. Although the majority of double eagles of the Coronet style were produced in large quantities, there are numerous rarities sprinkled throughout the series, with some issues being exceedingly rare.

The formation of a type set of new issues of gold coins introduced during the 1834-1900 span is a challenge. Happily, in grades from Very Fine to AU the challenge is realizable, and the result is a beautiful display covering one of the most important eras in our coinage history.

The rare 1883 $20 double eagle shown above is representative of the design minted from 1877 through 1907, with the denomination on the reverse spelled out as TWENTY DOLLARS.

GOLD DOLLAR
1849-1854 Liberty Head

Designed by: James Barton Longacre
Issue dates: 1849-1854
Composition: 0.900 part gold, 0.100 part copper
Diameter: 13 mm
Weight: 25.8 grains
Edge: Reeded
Business strike mintage: 12,565,273
Proof mintage: Fewer than 50

The gold dollar denomination made its debut in 1849. The obverse of the style minted from then to 1854 depicts the head of Miss Liberty facing left, her hair tied at the back, and wearing a coronet inscribed LIBERTY. Thirteen stars surround. The reverse depicts a wreath open at the top enclosing the numeral 1, the value DOLLAR, and the date. The inscription UNITED STATES OF AMERICA surrounds. Measuring just 13 mm in diameter, the gold dollar of the 1849-1854 type is the smallest United States coin, being even smaller than the 14 mm silver three-cent piece. Production was continuous from 1849 through 1854. Examples were produced primarily at the Philadelphia Mint, but the facilities at New Orleans, Dahlonega, Charlotte and San Francisco contributed as well. All of the Charlotte and Dahlonega coins are scarce today, and some are very rare.

The type set collector will probably want to acquire a Philadelphia Mint gold dollar in this span, for these are far more plentiful than those of branch mints and also are better struck. Charlotte and Dahlonega coins in particular are nearly always very weakly defined in certain areas. Examples of Philadelphia Mint gold dollars are readily available in various grades from Very Fine to AU. Uncirculated pieces are scarce, and superb Uncirculated coins are rare.

GOLD DOLLAR
1854-1856 Indian, Small Head

Designed by: James Barton Longacre
Issue dates: 1854-1856
Composition: 0.900 part gold, 0.100 part copper
Diameter: 15 mm
Weight: 25.8 grains
Edge: Reeded
Business strike mintage: 1,633,426
Proof mintage: Fewer than 50

In 1854 James B. Longacre restyled the gold dollar to an increased diameter. The obverse motif was changed to the head of an Indian princess, wearing a feather headdress and a band inscribed LIBERTY, facing left, with UNITED STATES OF AMERICA surrounding. The reverse shows a wreath of corn, cotton, wheat, and tobacco, similar to that used on the $3 of the same year (and the Flying Eagle cent minted later, beginning in 1856). From the very outset difficulties in striking ensued. The high relief of the head of Miss Liberty on the obverse caused the situation in which metal flowing into the deep die recess for the obverse prevented the relief areas on the corresponding part of the reverse, particularly the central two digits of the date, from striking up properly. Also there were problems with the striking up of the wreath and certain parts of Miss Liberty's head. After a coinage in 1854 at the Philadelphia Mint, a coinage in 1855 at the Philadelphia, Charlotte, Dahlonega, and New Orleans mints, and a coinage in 1856 at the San Francisco Mint only, the obverse motif was modified. In the 1854-1856 span there are several scarce issues and two rarities, the 1855-C and 1855-D.

The type collector will have no difficulty in encountering a Philadelphia Mint coin of 1854 or 1855 in any desired grade from Very Fine through AU. Uncirculated pieces are scarce, and superb Uncirculated coins are seldom met with. Nearly all pieces are lightly struck at the center of the date on the reverse, so this is to be expected. Indeed, this is the reason the design was changed in 1856. The 1854-1856 dollar, usually called the Type II, is the scarcest of the gold dollar designs and is the key to a gold dollar type set.

GOLD DOLLAR
1856-1889 Indian, Large Head

Designed by: James Barton Longacre
Issue dates: 1856-1889
Composition: 0.900 part gold, 0.100 part copper
Diameter: 15 mm
Weight: 25.8 grains
Edge: Reeded
Business strike mintage: 5,327,363
Proof mintage: 8,700 (estimated)

In 1856 James B. Longacre redesigned the gold dollar in an effort to create a motif that would strike up sharply and properly. The Indian princess style of Miss Liberty was continued, but in the new version the relief is lower and the details are different. Changes were also made in the reverse wreath. The result was a coin which indeed could be struck properly, with the result that gold dollars of the Type III design usually are well struck in most areas, including the central two digits of the date (the area which caused a problem on the preceding type). The Type III or Large Head motif was produced continuously from 1856 through 1889, although during and after the Civil War, mintages were exceedingly low for all years except a few. The nadir was touched in 1875 when just 400 business strikes and 20 Proofs were struck. Gold dollars were not popular with the public after the Civil War, and eventually the denomination was discontinued in 1889.

The type set collector can easily locate examples of the more plentiful dates in desired grades from Very Fine to AU. Uncirculated pieces are scarce, and superb Uncirculated are scarcer yet, although a flurry of investment and speculative activity which occurred among jewelers and numismatists during the 1879-1889 years resulted in the survival of more Uncirculated specimens of these dates than would otherwise have been the case. Proofs were minted of various Philadelphia Mint dates, with those struck from 1884 through 1889 being produced in relatively large quantities. Examples are fairly scarce today, however.

QUARTER EAGLE
1834-1839 Classic Head

Designed by: William Kneass
Issue dates: 1834-1839
Composition: 0.8992 part gold, 0.1008 part copper
Diameter: 18.2 mm
Weight: 64.5 grains
Edge: Reeded
Business strike mintage: 968,228
Proof mintage: Fewer than 50

Following the Act of June 28, 1834, which mandated a reduction in weight of gold coins, the quarter eagle was redesigned by Chief Engraver William Kneass. The new format, called the "Classic Head" by collectors today, features the head of Miss Liberty facing left, her hair secured by a band inscribed LIBERTY, stars circling her head, and with the date below. The reverse depicts an eagle with a shield on its breast, perched on an olive branch and holding three arrows. UNITED STATES OF AMERICA and 2½ D. surrounds. The motto E PLURIBUS UNUM, used on quarter eagles since 1796, was discontinued. Mintage quantities were large in the first several years of the coinage span, with the high water mark being 1836, when 547,986 were struck. In 1838, quarter eagles were struck at Charlotte for the first time, followed the next year by supplementary coinage at Dahlonega and New Orleans. By far the greatest number of 1834-1839 Classic Head quarter eagles were produced at Philadelphia.

Examples of this style can be obtained readily in grades from Fine through Extremely Fine. AU pieces are scarce, and Uncirculated pieces are scarcer yet. Superb Uncirculated coins are very rare. Uncirculated pieces of the first year of issue, 1834, often display proof-like surfaces.

QUARTER EAGLE
1840-1907 Coronet

Designed by: Christian Gobrecht
Issue dates: 1840-1907
Composition: 0.900 part gold, 0.100 part copper
Diameter: 18 mm
Weight: 64.5 grains
Edge: Reeded
Business strike mintage: 11,921,171
Proof mintage: 4,232 (estimated)

The Coronet motif, also called the Liberty Head or Braided Hair style, by Christian Gobrecht, appeared on the quarter eagle in 1840 and was continued uninterruptedly through 1907, the longest span in American coinage history of a design in use without major change or alterations. The obverse depicts Miss Liberty, her hair in a bun secured with a string of beads, wearing a coronet inscribed LIBER-TY, facing left, her head circled by stars, and with the date below. The reverse depicts an eagle with a shield on its breast, perched on an olive branch and holding three arrows. The inscription UNITED STATES OF AMERICA, 2½ D. surrounds. Throughout the coinage span 1840-1907 the Philadelphia Mint produced pieces each year. In general, early examples are fairly scarce, with the 1841 in particular being a prime rarity. Issues produced during the last decade of the series are those most often seen, with dates from 1902 through 1907 being the most plentiful. Additional coinage was accomplished from time to time at Charlotte, Dahlonega, San Francisco, and New Orleans.

The type set collector will encounter no difficulty in acquiring a representative specimen in any grade desired from Very Fine through AU. Uncirculated pieces are encountered with frequency, particularly those of the final years of the type. Superb Uncirculated pieces are available but are very scarce in relation to lower grades. Proofs were minted continuously, with the mintages crossing the 100 mark in later years. All Proofs are rare today.

$3 GOLD
1854-1889 Indian Head

Designed by: James Barton Longacre
Issue dates: 1854-1889
Composition: 0.900 part gold, 0.100 part copper
Diameter: 20.5 mm
Weight: 77.4 grains
Edge: Reeded
Business strike mintage: 538,074
Proof mintage: 2,060 (estimated)

The $3 pieces were first coined in 1854 and were produced at the Philadelphia Mint continuously through 1889. The obverse features the head of an Indian princess, facing left, wearing a feathered headdress upon which is a band inscribed LIBERTY. The inscription UNITED STATES OF AMERICA surrounds. The reverse displays an agricultural wreath enclosing 3 DOLLARS and the date. The obverse portrait and the reverse wreath are similar to those found on the Type II gold dollar minted 1854-1856, while the reverse wreath was later used on the Flying Eagle cents of 1856-1858. The $3 design was continued without major change from beginning to the end, except that issues of the year 1854 alone have the word DOLLARS in smaller letters than do the pieces from 1855 to 1889. In addition to the Philadelphia coinage, pieces were struck from time to time at Dahlonega, New Orleans (only in 1854) and San Francisco. All $3 issues are scarce. However, there will be no problem encountered in locating one of the higher mintage dates such as 1854, 1874, or 1878. Among coins of the 1854-1859 era, grades most often encountered range from Very Fine to Extremely Fine. AU pieces are scarce, and Uncirculated pieces are rare, with the possible exception of 1854, which occurs more frequently. Superb Uncirculated pieces are quite rare. Among later $3 pieces available grades are higher, with typical grades being in the Extremely Fine to AU range and, in the 1880s, AU to Uncirculated. Superb Uncirculated pieces are quite scarce. Proofs were minted and are available in proportion to their production figures. All are rare.

HALF EAGLE
1834-1838 Classic Head

Designed by: William Kneass
Issue dates: 1834-1838
Composition: 0.8992 part gold, 0.1008 part copper
Diameter: 22.5 mm
Weight: 129 grains
Edge: Reeded
Business strike mintage: 2,113,612
Proof mintage: Fewer than 50

Following the Act of June 28, 1834, which reduced the weight and composition of gold coins, the half eagle was redesigned by William Kneass, chief engraver at the Philadelphia Mint. Known as the "Classic Head" style, the new 1834 issue is a cousin to the quarter eagle of the same date. The obverse depicts the head of Miss Liberty facing left, her hair secured by a band inscribed LIBERTY, with stars circling her head, and with the date below. The reverse shows an eagle with a shield on its breast, perched on an olive branch and holding three arrows. The inscription UNITED STATES OF AMERICA, 5 D. surrounds. The motto E PLURIBUS UNUM, used earlier, was discontinued. Quarter eagles of this style were produced at the Philadelphia Mint continuously from 1834 through 1838 and at Charlotte and Dahlonega in 1838 only. Most of the mintage was accomplished at Philadelphia. Charlotte and Dahlonega pieces are rare.

The type set collector can readily obtain examples of Philadelphia issues in this span in grades from Very Fine to Extremely Fine. AU coins are scarce, Uncirculated pieces are elusive, and superb Uncirculated coins are very rare. Most examples are not sharply struck on the higher parts of the obverse.

HALF EAGLE
1839-1866 Coronet

Designed by: Christian Gobrecht
Issue dates: 1839-1866
Composition: 0.900 part gold, 0.100 part copper
Diameter: 22.5 mm (1839-1840); 21.6 mm (1840-1866)
Weight: 129.0 grains
Edge: Reeded
Business strike mintage: 9,114,049
Proof mintage: 450 (estimated)

Christian Gobrecht's Coronet design, also called the Liberty Head or Braided Hair type, made its appearance in the half eagle series in 1839. The obverse depicts a female head facing left, her hair tied in a bun secured by a string of beads, wearing a coronet inscribed LIBERTY, stars surrounding, and with the date below. The reverse shows an eagle with a shield on its breast, perched on an olive branch and holding three arrows. The inscription UNITED STATES OF AMERICA, FIVE D. surrounds. Issues of 1839 and some of 1840 measure 22.5 mm and are sometimes referred to as "broad mill" pieces, whereas later issues measure 21.6 mm. Coinage was accomplished at the Philadelphia Mint on a continuous basis during the span indicated. Additional pieces were made from time to time at Charlotte, Dahlonega, New Orleans, and San Francisco. In general, Charlotte and Dahlonega pieces are scarce. The prime rarity within the span is the 1854-S, struck during the first year of operation of the San Francisco Mint, a coin of which just 268 were made and of which only three are known to exist today.

The type set collector will have no problem acquiring one of the more plentiful dates in any desired grade from Very Fine through AU, with a typical grade encountered being Very Fine to Extremely Fine. Uncirculated pieces are scarce, and superb Uncirculated coins are very rare. Proofs were made in limited quantities and are rarities.

HALF EAGLE
1866-1908 Coronet, With Motto

Designed by: Christian Gobrecht
Issue dates: 1866-1908
Composition: 0.900 part gold, 0.100 part copper
Diameter: 21.6 mm
Weight: 129.0 grains
Edge: Reeded
Business strike mintage: 51,503,654
Proof mintage: 2,938

In 1866 the Coronet style was modified by adding the motto IN GOD WE TRUST on a ribbon above the eagle on the reverse. Apart from this, the motif with Liberty Head on the obverse and perched eagle on the reverse is the same used in earlier years. Mintage of the with-motto style was continuous at the Philadelphia Mint during the span indicated. Additional coins were made at San Francisco, Carson City, New Orleans, and, in 1906 and 1907, at the new Denver Mint.

The type set collector has a wide choice of issues in this span. Coins in grades from Very Fine to AU are readily encountered. Uncirculated pieces are plentiful as well. Superb Uncirculated coins are apt to be dated during the last decade of production and are considerably scarcer. Proofs were minted at Philadelphia and in each instance are rare.

EAGLE
1838-1866 Coronet

Designed by: Christian Gobrecht
Issue dates: 1838-1866
Composition: 0.900 part gold, 0.100 part copper
Diameter: 27 mm
Weight: 258 grains
Edge: Reeded
Business strike mintage: 5,292,499
Proof mintage: 400 (estimated)

Christian Gobrecht's Coronet style, also called the Liberty Head or Braided Hair motif, was used on the eagle beginning in 1838, two years earlier than on the quarter eagle and one year before the style was used on the half eagle. The obverse depicts a female head facing left, her hair in a bun secured by a string of beads, wearing a coronet inscribed LIBERTY. Stars surround, and the date is below. The reverse shows an eagle with a shield on its breast, perched on an olive branch, holding three arrows. The inscription UNITED STATES OF AMERICA, TEN D. surrounds. The Liberty head used in 1838 and early 1839 is slightly differently styled than that used later in 1839, continuing to the end of the series. The most prominent difference can be noted in the shape of the neck truncation. Mintages were continuous at the Philadelphia Mint. In addition, pieces were produced at New Orleans and San Francisco. A number of scarce issues occur in the span, with 1858 in particular considered to be rare.

For type set purposes the numismatist can readily obtain an example of one of the more plentiful dates in grades of Very Fine or Extremely Fine. AU pieces are scarcer, and Uncirculated pieces are quite scarce. Superb Uncirculated coins are seldom seen or encountered and are apt to come on the market only when great collections are marketed. Proofs were minted at Philadelphia and in all instances are rare.

EAGLE
1866-1907 Coronet, With Motto

Designed by: Christian Gobrecht
Issue dates: 1866-1907
Composition: 0.900 part gold, 0.100 part copper
Diameter: 27 mm
Weight: 258 grains
Edge: Reeded
Business strike mintage: 37,391,767
Proof mintage: 2,327

In 1866 the motto IN GOD WE TRUST was added to the reverse of the eagle and appears on a ribbon or scroll from that time through 1907. Otherwise the Liberty Head obverse and perched eagle reverse are the same as employed earlier. Production was continuous at the Philadelphia Mint during this span and nearly continuous at San Francisco. Beginning in 1870, examples were struck at the Carson City Mint. New Orleans coins were produced from 1879 through 1883 and again in several later years. Coins were struck at Denver in 1906 and 1907.

In grades from Very Fine to AU the type set collector will have a wide choice of specimens. Examples are not rare. Uncirculated pieces are readily encountered of dates toward the end of the type. Superb Uncirculated pieces are very elusive. Proofs were minted and are occasionally available; all are rare.

DOUBLE EAGLE
1849-1866 Coronet

Designed by: James Barton Longacre
Issue dates: 1849 (pattern); 1850-1866
Composition: 0.900 part gold, 0.100 part copper
Diameter: 34 mm
Weight: 516 grains
Edge: Reeded
Business strike mintage: 23,526,676
Proof mintage: 375 (estimated)

Following a pattern coinage in 1849, the double eagle or $20 gold made its debut in circulation in 1850. Designed by James B. Longacre, the obverse features the compact head of Miss Liberty, her hair tied in a bun, wearing a coronet inscribed LIBERTY. Stars surround, and the date is below. The motif is similar to that used on the gold dollars of 1849-1854. The reverse is a new motif not used elsewhere on American coinage and consists of an eagle with a squared-off shield on its breast, holding an olive branch and arrows, with ornaments to the left and right, stars and rays above, with the inscription UNITED STATES OF AMERICA, TWENTY D. surrounding. Double eagles of this type were made in large quantities from 1850 onward, although the span is sprinkled with scarce and rare issues.

The type collector will have no difficulty acquiring an example of one of the more plentiful dates in Very Fine to Extremely Fine preservation. AU pieces are scarce. Uncirculated pieces are very scarce, and superb Uncirculated coins are exceedingly rare, although occasionally pieces dated 1861 come on the market. Early San Francisco Mint issues, 1854-S through 1857-S, are sometimes seen with lightly etched surfaces. Such pieces were recovered from shipwrecks and spent a century or more subjected to the effects of salt water. Proofs in all instances are exceedingly rare.

DOUBLE EAGLE
1866-1876 Coronet, With Motto

Designed by: James Barton Longacre
Issue dates: 1866-1876
Composition: 0.900 part gold, 0.100 part copper
Diameter: 30 mm
Weight: 516 grains
Edge: Reeded
Business strike mintage: 16,160,758
Proof mintage: 335

In 1866 the reverse of the Coronet or Liberty Head style was modified by adding the motto IN GOD WE TRUST within the circle of stars above the eagle. This motto was continued from this point forward. The type minted from 1866 through 1876 is defined by the combination of the IN GOD WE TRUST motto with the denomination below expressed as TWENTY D. In 1877 the denomination was expressed differently, thus isolating the earlier issues as a distinct type. Production was continuous at the Philadelphia and San Francisco mints. Carson City coins were produced beginning in 1870, with 1870-CC being a rarity today.

The type set collector can readily obtain examples of commoner issues in grades from Very Fine to Extremely Fine or AU. Uncirculated pieces are quite scarce, and superb Uncirculated coins are exceedingly rare. Proofs are very rare.

DOUBLE EAGLE
1877-1907 Coronet, TWENTY DOLLARS

Designed by: James Barton Longacre
Issue dates: 1877-1907
Composition: 0.900 part gold, 0.100 part copper
Diameter: 30 mm
Weight: 516 grains
Edge: Reeded
Business strike mintage: 64,137,477
Proof mintage: 2,426

The Coronet or Liberty Head obverse motif was continued during the 1877-1907 span, as was the reverse with IN GOD WE TRUST above the eagle. However, the denomination, formerly expressed as TWENTY D., was changed to read TWENTY DOLLARS, thus creating a new type. Examples were produced continuously at Philadelphia and intermittently at Carson City and San Francisco. New Orleans produced double eagles of this style in 1879, and pieces were struck at Denver in 1906 and 1907. There are a number of rare issues within the span, with the 1883 and 1884 Philadelphia coins being legendary in this regard.

The type set collector will have no difficulty obtaining a representative example in any grade from Very Fine to AU, with Extremely Fine and AU pieces being abundant. Uncirculated pieces are scarcer and when seen are apt to be dated during the last decade of production. Superb Uncirculated pieces are scarcer yet and when found are apt to be dated 1904. Proofs in all instances are rare.

Chapter 11

New Issues
GOLD
1901-1933

Gold coin designs introduced during the 1901-1933 period are closely grouped around the years 1907-1908 and in each instance are related to noted sculptor Augustus Saint-Gaudens. The $10 eagle and $20 double eagle of 1907 are each from his hand. After his death in the summer of that year, Boston sculptor Bela Lyon Pratt, who studied with Saint-Gaudens, picked up the traces and composed new designs for the $2½ and $5 values.

The story of Saint-Gaudens' involvement with American coinage is a long and romantic one and is recounted in numerous places, including the present author's book, *United States Gold Coins: An Illustrated History*. Saint-Gaudens, was a personal acquaintance of President Theodore Roosevelt. One day, while at the Smithsonian Institution, Roosevelt saw a group of Greek coins and was impressed by their artistry and sculptured appearance. By comparison the current American coinage was very bland, he thought. His thinking continued on the subject, and soon he contacted Saint-Gaudens and asked him if he would redesign the *entire* American coinage, from the cent through the double eagle. In the early years, Saint-Gaudens had achieved international renown for many of his medallic and sculptural works, including the figure of Diana atop Madison Square Garden, the Shaw Memorial in Boston, the Sherman Victory Monument in New York City's Central Park, and other efforts. Earlier, Saint-Gaudens maintained studios in New York City, later moving to a hillside location overlooking the Connecticut River Valley in Cornish, New Hampshire, where he established a studio in a verdant setting near his home, "Aspet." Today, the Saint-Gaudens National Historic Site is maintained by the National Parks Service and is open to the public.

Saint-Gaudens studied the earlier American coinage and expressed the opinion to Roosevelt that the finest design to that point was the flying eagle as used on the cents of 1856-1858. Sketches were prepared for several denominations, including the cent, $10, and $20. The reverse of the latter denomination used a modified version of the flying eagle that Saint-Gaudens admired from earlier times.

For the double eagle, Saint-Gaudens used as a central motif the figure of Victory, said to have been modeled by his mistress, Davida Clark, which was used earlier on the Sherman Monument. The reverse, as noted, illustrated the flying eagle design. Early versions of the double eagle expressed the date in Roman numerals, MCMVII, and were done in very high relief, more like a medal than a coin, with a sculptured effect. All the while, Saint-Gaudens maintained close contact with President Roosevelt. The Philadelphia Mint was not consulted.

Charles E. Barber, chief engraver at the Philadelphia Mint, became angry, for at that time the design of new coinage was the provenance of the Mint staff. Indeed, the coins then in circulation—ranging from the Indian cent to the Liberty Head $20—were all designed by past or present Mint employees. When Barber learned of the high-relief format of the new double eagle, he immediately and rightly stated that such would not be compatible with high-speed production presses. Angered, President Roosevelt said that this design must be used anyway, even if only double eagle *per day* could be struck! He called the interference with the Mint's coinage prerogative his "pet crime." To satisfy Roosevelt, 11,250 examples of the MCMVII High Relief double were struck, laboriously on a medal press, requiring three impressions per coin. After that, Chief Engraver Barber prevailed, the design was severely modified, and later issues were produced with the date in Arabic numerals, such as 1907, and in shallow relief. The modified Saint-Gaudens' design was used through the end of the series in 1933.

Early double eagles lacked the motto IN GOD WE TRUST, which had been used on the denomination since 1866, for President Roosevelt felt that God's name appearing on circulating money was sacrilegious. Subsequently, Congress overruled the president, and IN GOD WE TRUST was added to the reverse of the double eagle part way through 1908. The motto addition was performed on the eagle at the same time.

The eagle or $10 gold of 1907, also designed by Saint-Gaudens, featured a head copied from a portrait bust, also of Davida Clark. The idea of outfitting Miss Liberty, a lady, with an Indian headdress typically worn by *male* Indians caused some comment at the time, but the controversy was soon forgotten.

By the time of Saint-Gaudens' death in 1907, only the $10 and $20 denominations had been modeled. Accordingly, President

Bela Lyon Pratt's innovative design for $2½ and $5 (a $5 is shown above) pieces, minted from 1908 through 1929, featured the motifs incuse or sunken in the coin, with the field or background, normally the lowest part of a coin's design, being the highest part.

The Indian $10 motif, by Augustus Saint-Gaudens, is illustrated above with a 1930-S issue, one of the prime rarities in the series.

Roosevelt's dream of having the artist redesign the entire coinage spectrum fell short of the mark.

In 1908, Bela Lyon Pratt redesigned the gold quarter eagle and half eagle, producing an innovative motif featuring an Indian on the obverse and a perched eagle on the reverse, with the designs and inscriptions all incuse or recessed in the surface, a radical departure from earlier United States circulating coinage. The highest areas of the new coins were the fields, traditionally the lowest areas on other coins. The incuse designs of Pratt were used from 1908 through 1929.

The formation of a *basic* type set of new gold coin designs of the early 20th century will present no problem. Such a six-piece set would include one example each of the Indian quarter eagle and half eagle, a 1907-1908 Saint-Gaudens $10 without IN GOD WE TRUST and a 1908-1933 specimen with the motto; a 1907-1908 Saint-Gaudens $20 without the motto and a later dated specimen with IN GOD WE TRUST. Examples are readily found in grades from Very Fine to AU. Uncirculated pieces are scarce, and superb Uncirculated pieces are quite scarce.

If the MCMVII High Relief double eagle is added, making a total of seven coins in the set, then this one piece will form a special challenge. There are hundreds of specimens in numismatic hands, but the popularity of them is such that they are quite expensive in relation to the other coins of the set.

QUARTER EAGLE
1908-1929 Indian

Designed by: Bela Lyon Pratt
Issue dates: 1908-1929
Composition: 0.900 part gold, 0.100 part copper
Diameter: 18 mm
Weight: 64.5 grains
Edge: Reeded
Business strike mintage: 7,250,261
Proof mintage: 1,827

In 1908 numismatists were surprised by the advent of the new quarter eagle and half eagle designed by sculptor Bela Lyon Pratt, for no advance notice had been released concerning them. A departure from the procedure used earlier in United States coinage, the new design features were recessed or incuse in the coins, with the field of the pieces, normally the lowest part, being the highest part. The obverse of the Pratt quarter eagle, known as the Indian Head type, features an Indian chief facing left, with LIBERTY above, six stars to the left and seven to the right, and the date below. The reverse shows an eagle perched on a branch or log, with UNITED STATES OF AMERICA above, E PLURIBUS UNUM to the left, IN GOD WE TRUST to the right, and the denomination expressed as 2½ DOLLARS below. Examples were produced at the Phildelphia Mint from 1908 through 1915 and again from 1925 through 1929. Denver Mint pieces were produced in 1911, 1914 and 1925, with the 1911-D considered to be the rarity of the series.

The type set collector can easily find examples of the Indian Head quarter eagle in grades from Very Fine to AU. Uncirculated pieces are scarce, and superb Uncirculated pieces are very scarce. The scarcity of higher grade pieces is explained not by the mintages, which in most instances were generous, but by the format of the coin. The field of a typical coin, exposed to wear and other effects, acquired marks quickly, and even storage in a mint bag was apt to reduce the grade of a piece below the Uncirculated level.

HALF EAGLE
1908-1929 Indian

Designed by: Bela Lyon Pratt
Issue dates: 1908-1929
Composition: 0.900 part gold, 0.100 part copper
Diameter: 21.6 mm
Weight: 129 grains
Edge: Reeded
Business strike mintage: 14,078,066
Proof mintage: 1,077

Bela Lyon Pratt's innovative Indian Head half eagle follows the format of the related quarter eagle and features all of the design recessed or incuse in the coin's surface, with the field, normally the lowest part on a coin, being the highest part. As is the case with quarter eagles, mintmarks are raised and in relief. The obverse depicts an Indian chief facing left, LIBERTY above, six stars to the left and seven to the right, and the date below. The reverse shows an eagle perched on a branch or a log with UNITED STATES OF AMERICA above, E PLURIBUS UNUM to the left, IN GOD WE TRUST to the right, and the denomination expressed as FIVE DOLLARS below. Mintage was accomplished at Philadelphia from 1908 through 1915 and again in 1929. Denver struck half eagles of this type from 1909 through 1911 and again in 1914. San Francisco half eagles were made from 1908 through 1916. At New Orleans the Indian quarter eagle was struck in one year only, 1909, the last year of operation of that minting facility.

The availability of Indian Head quarter eagles to the type set collector is similar to that of related quarter eagles. Examples in grades from Very Fine to AU are easily obtained. Uncirculated pieces are scarce, and superb Uncirculated coins are seldom seen. The rarity of upper echelon grades is explained by a characteristic of the coin's surface. The field, being the highest part, quickly acquired marks and abrasions, even while stored in mint bags before being released into circulation.

EAGLE
1907-1908 Indian, No Motto

Designed by: Augustus Saint-Gaudens
Issue dates: 1907-1908
Composition: 0.900 part gold, 0.100 part copper
Diameter: 27 mm
Weight: 258 grains
Edge: 46 raised stars
Business strike mintage: 483,448
Proof mintage: None of regular issue

Following the coinage of two varieties of experimental pieces, with periods before and after the legends on the reverse, business strikes of the 1907-1908 issue were produced for circulation. The obverse depicts Miss Liberty wearing an Indian headdress inscribed LIBERTY on a band, 13 stars are in an arc above, and the date is below. The reverse depicts a perched eagle with UNITED STATES OF AMERICA above, the motto E PLURIBUS UNUM to the right, and the denomination expressed as TEN DOLLARS below. As President Roosevelt personally objected to the use of the name of the Diety on coins, the Indian issues of 1907 and certain issues of 1908 lack IN GOD WE TRUST. Coinage of the type was effected at Philadelphia in 1907 and 1908 and also in Denver the latter year.

Specimens are readily available in grades from Extremely Fine to AU. Uncirculated pieces are seen with some regularity, but superb Uncirculated coins are decidedly rare.

EAGLE
1908-1933 Indian, With Motto

Designed by: Augustus Saint-Gaudens
Issue dates: 1908-1933
Composition: 0.900 part gold, 0.100 part copper
Diameter: 27 mm
Weight: 258 grains
Edge: 46 stars 1908-1911; 48 stars 1912-1933
Business strike mintage: 14,385,139
Proof mintage: 768

In 1908 Saint-Gaudens' Indian Head design was modified on the reverse by the addition of IN GOD WE TRUST in the field at the center right. The motto, restored by a special act of Congress, remained in effect through the end of the series in 1933. Otherwise the Indian head obverse and perched eagle reverse motif remained unchanged. The edges of issues 1908-1911 have 46 raised stars, while those minted from 1912 onward have 48 raised stars, reflecting an increased number of states in the Union. Mintage was intense and continuous from 1908 through 1916, after which no examples were made until 1920-S, followed by a gap until the 1926 Philadelphia issue, with the next following being 1930-S, then 1932 and 1933.

The numismatist seeking an example of the 1908-1933 type will have no difficulty locating one of the more plentiful dates in Extremely Fine to AU grade. Uncirculated pieces are fairly scarce, with the exception of 1926 and in particular 1932. Superb Uncirculated pieces dated 1926 and 1932 are rare, and superb Uncirculated pieces of other dates are very rare. In general, much of the mintage from 1908 through 1916 was used extensively in bank to bank transactions and overseas, with the result that most of these seen today show signs of wear.

DOUBLE EAGLE
MCMVII (1907) High Relief

Designed by: Augustus Saint-Gaudens
Issue date: 1907
Composition: 0.900 part gold, 0.100 part copper
Diameter: 34 mm
Weight: 516 grains
Edge: Lettered E PLURIBUS UNUM with stars interspersing
Business strike mintage: 11,250
Proof mintage: Fewer than 25

In 1907 fewer than two dozen examples of the new Saint-Gaudens design were made in *Extremely* High Relief with concave fields; pieces considered today to be patterns. Following that, pieces in slightly lower relief, but still with a sculptured effect and in high relief compared earlier later issues, known today as High Relief issues, were produced to the extent of 11,250 for circulation. After the relatively small mintage was accomplished, the High Relief format was discontinued. The obverse of this style depicts Miss Liberty striding forward with radiant sun rays behind and a distant view of the Capitol building, with LIBERTY above and the date expressed as MCMVII in the lower right field. The reverse shows an eagle flying left, Saint-Gaudens' updated version of that found on Flying Eagle cents of the 1856-1858 era, with UNITED STATES OF AMERICA and TWENTY DOLLARS in two lines above. Below is the sun with resplendent rays.

Although 11,250 pieces were struck for circulation, from the very outset these coins sold at a premium and were recognized as collectors' items. As a result, most of the several hundred or more pieces surviving today are in higher grades, primarily About Uncirculated and Uncirculated. Truly superb Uncirculated pieces, without any trace of rubbing on the higher obverse parts, are rare.

DOUBLE EAGLE
1907-1908 No Motto

Designed by: Augustus Saint-Gaudens
Issue dates: 1907-1908
Composition: 0.900 part gold, 0.100 part copper
Diameter: 34 mm
Weight: 516 grains
Edge: Lettered E PLURIBUS UNUM
Business strike mintage: 5,294,968
Proof mintage: Fewer than 5

After the High Relief MCMVII pieces had been struck, the design was modified under the direction of Charles E. Barber at the Philadelphia Mint, and subsequent issues featured shallow relief and the date in Arabic numerals. The first style minted, that produced at the Philadelphia Mint in 1907 and 1908 and in Denver in 1908, lacks the motto IN GOD WE TRUST, for President Theodore Roosevelt personally objected to it. The general design remains the same as on the High Relief issues and depicts Miss Liberty striding forward, with rays and the Capitol building in the background, LIBERTY above, and the date, now expressed in Arabic numerals, to the lower right. The reverse is similar and depicts an eagle flying to the left over the sun, with UNITED STATES OF AMERICA and TWENTY DOLLARS in two lines above. Around the obverse border of all Saint-Gaudens $20 issues is a circle of stars, 46 stars on those minted from 1907 through 1911 and 48 stars on those made from 1912 through 1933.

Examples of the 1907-1908 No Motto style are readily obtained in grades from Extremely Fine to AU. Uncirculated pieces are encountered with some frequency, but superb Uncirculated coins are decidedly scarce.

DOUBLE EAGLE
1908-1933 With Motto

Designed by: Augustus Saint-Gaudens
Issue dates: 1908-1933
Composition: 0.900 part gold, 0.100 part copper
Diameter: 34 mm
Weight: 516 grains
Edge: Lettered E PLURIBUS UNUM
Business strike mintage: 64,981,428
Proof mintage: 687

In 1908 the Saint-Gaudens design was modified by adding IN GOD WE TRUST in an arc just above the sun on the reverse. Otherwise the design is the same as the preceding. Issues minted from 1908 through 1911 have 46 stars around the obverse border, while those minted from 1912 through 1933 have 48 stars, reflecting a larger number of states in the Union. Production was accomplished on a fairly continuous basis from 1908 through 1933. Despite high mintages, certain issues of the 1920s are rare, for many were simply stored by the Treasury Department and then melted following the 1933 gold recall. The design of the issue features Miss Liberty on the obverse and a flying eagle on the reverse and is similar to that of 1907-1908 except for the addition of the motto.

The type set collector will encounter no difficulty finding a specimen in Extremely Fine to AU grade. Uncirculated coins are relatively plentiful, but superb Uncirculated pieces are elusive. In general, issues from 1908 through 1921 are very rare in superb Uncirculated condition, while certain issues of the 1920s, particularly Philadelphia Mint coins from 1924 to 1928, are more readily obtained, but still they present a challenge.

Chapter 12

Some Interesting Options

As mentioned on page 17, type sets come in many different varieties, and there is no such thing as an "official" or a "standard" type set. The pieces listed in the preceding chapters of the present volume are those which have been most popular with collectors in the past. A good case can be made for incorporating certain other issues as well, and several of these are illustrated on the following pages.

CENTS

1793-1795 Liberty Cap, Lettered Edge

Designed by: John Gardner
Issue dates: 1793-1795
Composition: Copper
Diameter: Average 29 mm
Weight: 208 grains
Edge: ONE HUNDRED FOR A DOLLAR.
Business strike mintage: 966,577
Proof mintage: None

1795-1796 Liberty Cap, Plain Edge

Designed by: John Gardner
Issue dates: 1795-1796
Composition: Copper
Diameter: Average 29 mm
Weight: 168 grains
Edge: Plain
Business strike mintage: 611,325
Proof mintage: None

On page 42 of the present book is a combined listing for the 1793-1796 Liberty Cap cent, with the notation that early pieces have the edge lettered ONE HUNDRED FOR A DOLLAR, and later pieces have plain edges. On the present page we have divided this type into two categories and have listed the characteristics for each.

HALF DISME
1792

Designed by: William Russell Birch?
Issue date: 1792
Composition: 0.8924 silver, 0.1076 copper
Diameter: 17.5 mm
Weight: 20.8 grains
Edge: Diagonally reeded
Business strike mintage: 1,000-2,000 pieces
Proof mintage: None

For many years numismatists have considered the 1792 half disme to be a pattern. However, a case can be made for its status as a regular issue. In his fourth annual address, November 6, 1792, President George Washington mentioned that national coinage had commenced: "There has been a small beginning in the coinage of half dismes; the want of small coins in circulation calling the first attention to them." This should satisfy any doubters as to the intention of the coinage.

In his *Complete Encyclopedia of U.S. and Colonial Coins*, Walter Breen, using certain information unearthed by Robert W. Julian, states that Mint Director David Rittenhouse wrote to Washington on July 9, 1792, asking for and subsequently receiving permission to strike cents and small silver coins. On July 13, Adam Eckfeldt and other workmen hired for the Mint struck 1,500 half dismes from dies prepared by Birch. The identity of Birch has been a matter of discussion among numismatists, and various candidates have been advanced, including Thomas Birch and William Russell Birch. Carl W. Carlson in an article in *The Numismatist* in 1982 presented a case for William Russell Birch, a British engraver.

These 1792 half dismes were struck in conformity to the Mint Act of April 2, 1792, and were official federal issues, although at the time they were made the facilities were not in place at the Philadelphia Mint. It is believed that the striking took place in the cellar of John Harper, a saw maker at Sixth and Cherry streets, not far from the Mint site.

Today possibly 100 or so 1792 half dismes survive, nearly all of which show extensive signs of wear. Examples in grades of AU or finer are extreme rarities.

SILVER DOLLAR
1836

Designed by: Christian Gobrecht
Issue dates: 1836-1837
Composition: 0.8924 silver, 0.1076 copper, 1836; 0.900 silver,
    0.100 copper, 1837.
Diameter: 39 mm
Weight: 416 grains, 1836; 412.5 grains, 1837.
Edge: Plain
Business strike mintage: None
Proof mintage: 1,600 (plus restrikes)

In 1835, Chief Engraver Christian Gobrecht embarked on a redesigning of silver motifs. In 1836 the first "Liberty Seated" design appeared in coinage form. The reverse depicted a flying eagle. The initial pattern issue had the inscription C. GOBRECHT F. in the field between the date and the base of Miss Liberty. The engraver's signature was subsequently relocated to the base of Miss Liberty itself, after which time this design was used for circulation. On December 31, 1836, warrants authorized the delivery of a total of 1,000 of these dollars to the Bank of the United States. These pieces were made to the current weight standard of 416 grains. On March 31, 1837, 600 further dollars were minted, with the 1836 date, and also went into circulation, these latter pieces being 412.5 grains, the new standard in use following the Act of January 18, 1837. The 1,000 pieces issued in 1836 have the dies aligned in normal fashion (the obverse and reverse 180° apart), while those minted in 1837 have the obverse and reverse aligned in the same direction. In addition, some restrikes were made at a later date, possibly 1858-1860, and these have the obverse and reverse dies aligned nearly in the same direction, the difference being that on these restrikes the eagle is flying horizontally rather than slightly upward. The quantity of restrikes minted is not known.

SILVER DOLLAR
1839

Designed by: Christian Gobrecht
Issue date: 1839
Composition: 0.900 silver, 0.100 copper
Diameter: 39 mm
Weight: 412.5 grains
Edge: Reeded
Business strike mintage: None
Proof mintage: 300 plus restrikes

The 1839 Gobrecht dollar listed here is somewhat similar to the preceding 1836 issue, but with notable differences, including the addition of stars of obverse, deletion of stars from the reverse, and the incorporation of a reeded edge.

On December 31, 1839, the chief coiner of the Philadelphia Mint delivered 300 silver dollars, all with the Proof finish. Most of these were placed into circulation. The year previous, 1838, saw the production of patterns of this design, but, so far as is known, none of the 1838 issues were put into circulation at the time, so they are not listed here.

In addition to the 300 "originals" reported to have been coined, a number of restrikes were made. However, fewer restrikes seem to exist today of 1839 than of 1836, and as a date the 1839 is considerably rarer.

Bibliography

A good reference library is a wonderful key to the appreciation of a type set collection. Each design type has its own story to tell. The enjoyment of any coin can be enhanced by reading about its history. The following books on specialized series and denominations are especially helpful.

Adams, John W. (editor), *Monographs on Varieties of U.S. Large Cents 1793-1794*. An anthology of articles concerning the two earliest dates in the large cent series, the romance, history, rarity, etc. A delightful volume for the specialist.

Ahwash, Kamal M., *Encyclopedia of United States Liberty Seated Dimes 1837-1891*. A large and extensively illustrated volume covering the subject indicated.

Akers, David W., *U.S. Gold Coins*—a series of separate volumes covering gold dollars, quarter eagles, $3 and $4 pieces, half eagles, eagles, and double eagles, with a page or more devoted to each variety, and with data concerning the frequency of appearance of each at auction, the availability in certain grades, etc. A very valuable reference set for the advanced numismatist.

Beistle, M.L., *Register of United States Half Dollar Die Varieties and Sub-Varieties*. A 1929 volume, the predecessor of the later Overton work on the subject, discussing die varieties. The text is particularly valuable for the issues 1794-1836, but useful data on later issues can be found as well.

Bolender, M.H., *U.S. Early Silver Dollars*. The standard reference describing die varieties of silver dollars of the 1794-1803 years.

Bowers, Q. David, *The History of United States Coinage*. Illustrated by the $25 million Garrett Collection, this large volume, written for The Johns Hopkins University, covers all there is of United States coinage, minting, and history.

Bowers, Q. David, *U.S. Gold Coins: An Illustrated History*. Illustrated by the $12 million Eliasberg Collection of gold coins, this volume covers all American gold issues from dollars through double eagles, with the history and background of each series and design, and with information concerning collecting over the years, various rarities, etc. A standard reference.

Bowers, Q. David, *United States Copper Coins: An Action Guide for the Collector and Investor*. A book covering copper issues including half cents, large cents, small cents, and two cent pieces, illustrating major types and discussing rarities, the availability of certain issues, and other useful information.

Bowers, Q. David, *United Stated Dimes, Quarters, and Half Dollars: An Action Guide for the Collector and Investor.* A detailed discussion of these series.

Bowers, Q. David, *United States Three-Cent and Five-Cent Coins: An Action Guide for the Collector and Investor.* A detailed discussion of nickel and silver three-cent pieces, nickel five-cent pieces (of all types from Shield through Jefferson issues), and half dimes. Various types, varieties, historical items, etc. are discussed, and many collecting hints and tips are given.

Bowers & Ruddy Galleries, Inc., *The United States Gold Collection.* 1982 auction catalogue of the Louis Eliasberg Collection offering one of each date and mintmark issue of United States gold coins from dollars to double eagles.

Breen, Walter, *Walter Breen's Encyclopedia of United States Half Cents 1793-1857.* A marvelous volume detailing all aspects of half cent numismatology, accompanied by superb photographs (taken by Jack Collins) and an interesting, if often opinionated text. A rather extensive volume which will tell you all you want to know about half cents, and probably quite a bit you never dreamed of asking about!

Breen, Walter, *United States Half Dimes, A Supplement.* 1958 monograph supplementing the 1931 D.W. Valentine's book on the subject.

Breen, Walter, *Walter Breen's Complete Encyclopedia of U.S. and Colonial Coins,* 1988. A landmark volume with detailed information on all United States series, a book which caused a sensation when it was published and which is today a key volume in any serious United States numismatic library.

Browning, A.W., *The Early Quarters of the United States.* The classic reference describing die varieties of early quarter dollars prior to the Liberty Seated type.

Cohen, Roger S., Jr., *American Half Cents, The ''Little Half Sisters.''* A good general guide to half cent die varieties of the 1793-1857 years, the "last word" on the subject until Walter Breen's book came along in 1983.

Davis, David, and several other authors, *Early United States Dimes 1796-1837.* A marvelously detailed guide to dimes in this date range, with descriptions concerning known die varieties. The standard reference in the field.

Dryfhout, John H., *The Work of Augustus Saint-Gaudens.* Not a numismatic book but, rather, a biography of Saint-Gaudens and a delination of his various sculptures, plaques, and other efforts. Excellent background information for the $10 and $20 gold coinage of 1907.

Durst, Sanford (editor), *Early American Coppers.* A collection of articles pertaining to United States large cents, half cents, and related matters. Written by many authors. A volume for the specialist.

Ehrmantraut, Jack A., Jr., *An Analysis of Gem Franklin Half Dollars.* A discussion pertaining to various Franklin half dollars 1948-1963, with comments concerning the availability of each.

Ganz, David L., *The world of Coins and Coin Collection.* New York: Charles Scribner's Sons, 1985.

Kliman, Myron M., *The Two Cent Piece and Varieties.* A monograph, published in 1977, detailing two-cent pieces from 1864 to 1873 and discussing the die varieties within the series.

Lapp, Warren A. and Herbert A. Silberman (editors), *United States Large Cents, 1793-1857.* An anthology containing over 100 articles by various authors, published in *The Numismatist* between 1895 and 1971, pertaining to large cents and half cents. A great volume for the specialist.

Loring, Denis (editor), *Monographs on Varieties of U.S. Large Cents 1795-1803.* Many different articles on the subject indicated. Fascinating reading for the specialist.

Miller, Wayne, *The Morgan and Peace Dollar Textbook.* A detailed discussion of the mintage, striking, and availability of various silver dollars 1878-1935. A very useful and popular book.

Nagengast, Bernard, *The Jefferson Nickel Analyst*. A monograph covering the various issues of Jefferson nickels from 1938 onward, with particular relation to the availability of sharply struck examples of certain dates and mintmarks. Surprisingly, certain common issues are great rarities so far as sharply struck pieces are concerned.

Newcomb, Howard R., *United States Copper Cents, 1816-1857*. The standard guide to die varieties of later large cents, 1816-1857. Little editorial or "reading" material is included. Valuable for the painstaking, detailed listings of die varieties.

Overton, Al C., *Early Half Dollar Die Varieties 1794-1836*. A detailed illustrated volume pertaining to die varieties of the years indicated. The standard reference.

Radeker, William D., *Collecting Coins by Designs: A Type Collector's Handbook*. Short essays, thoughts, and ideas on collecting by design types presented in the form of a monograph.

Reiver, Jules, *Variety Identification Manual for U.S. Half Dimes 1794-1837*. A key and quick index, plus rarity ratings, to D.W. Valentine's classic half dime book.

Sheldon, Dr. William H., *Penny Whimsy*. The standard text on United States large cents of the years 1793-1814. A book which goes far beyond the large cent area and discusses many aspects such as markets, grading, psychology of collecting, etc. A highly recommended and very basic text. A numismatic classic.

Stack, Norman, *United States Type Coins*. A very nice "portfolio," illustrated in color, of various designs from the earliest years onward.

Stewart, Frank H., *History of the First U.S. Mint*. A view of the operations of the Philadelphia Mint in the early days.

Swiatek, Anthony, *The Walking Liberty Half Dollar*. A 72-page monograph discussing one of America's most popular series, half dollars of the 1916-1947 years.

Taxay, Don, *U.S. Mint and Coinage*. A superb book which is a "must" for every collector of coins by design type. Detailed information concerning the operations of the early Philadelphia Mint, combined with much valuable data pertaining to artists, engravers, and new designs over the years.

Valentine, D.W., *The United States Half Dimes*, published by the American Numismatic Society, 1931, later reprinted. The basic guide to half dime die varieties. Particularly valuable for issues 1794-1837, but useful for certain later issues as well. A standard reference.

Van Allen, Leroy, and A. George Mallis, *Morgan & Peace Silver Dollars*. A large book describing in detail the background and production of Morgan and Peace dollars, minting and melting, and with an incredibly detailed listing of minute die varieties.

Willem, John M., *The United States Trade Dollar*. A detailed study of the trade dollar, with emphasis on historical background.

White, Weimar W., *The Liberty Seated Dollar 1840-1873*. A monograph with a grading commentary, investment ideas and theories, and comments by date.

Yeoman, Richard S., *A Guide Book of United States Coins*. The *standard reference* on United States coins, and one of the ten best-selling books in general publishing history. A wonderful overview of American coinage from the earliest years onward.

Index

Index